The

 DEEPER SECRET

The DEEPER SECRET

ANNEMARIE POSTMA

Wanting, deciding, and taking responsibility
are personal choices that create miracles.

ANNEMARIE POSTMA

ABOUT THE AUTHOR

Life Science author Annemarie Postma (1969) studied law and later became the first professional European model with a handicap. In 1995, she was featured in *Playboy*, which resulted in her becoming a sought-after guest on national and international talk shows. Since then she has developed into a successful publicist and writer, specializing in self-esteem and self-respect—the two aspects at the absolute core of contemporary self-development, according to Annemarie.

Annemarie has reached hundreds of thousands of readers with her books *I Love Me, Making Love,* and *The Body Is Perfect.* Her books, passionate, holistic vision of life is characterized in all her work, in which she tackles the questions "How can I learn to truly live? How can I create the life that is best for me?" Annemarie sees mental, physical, emotional, and spiritual health as inextricably linked to one another. Since February 2005, Annemarie has been goodwill ambassador of the Netherlands Foundation for Handicapped Children (NSGK).

Annemarie was eleven years old when, as a result of a tick bite that was not discovered in time, partial paraplegia changed her life. Now she shares her experiences and the insights she has gained in her books, workshops, and lectures. Her passion for life, love of reality, and social involvement make her a source of inspiration for many people.

www.thedeepersecret.nl
www.ankhhermes.nl

First edition published in Holland
by Uitgeverij Ankh-Hermes bv, Deventer, 2008

This edition published in the UK 2009 by
Watkins Publishing, Sixth Floor, Castle House,
75–76 Wells Street, London W1T 3QH

1 3 5 7 9 10 8 6 4 2

Designed by Jen Cogliantry
Typeset by Jen Cogliantry

Printed and bound in Great Britain

British Library Cataloguing-in-Publication Data Available

ISBN: 978-1-906787-23-3
www.watkinspublishing.co.uk

Contents

PREFACE

If there is something you need,
it will come to you, on the condition
that you are free. That is the cosmic law.

INTI CESAR MELASQUEZ

*W*herever you go, everyone is talking about *The Secret*. This is not surprising, because *The Secret* explains that to get what you most desire, you need only know what it is, and that simply by thinking of what you want, you will attract the life of your dreams.

The Secret is about the law of attraction—a fundamental law of nature and one that I have been writing about for years. We do attract the circumstances of our own lives, because we create a large part of our outer world from our inner world. In fact, we are continually creating, often without realizing it. Thought by thought we give shape to our existence, and whatever we direct our attention to will grow—for good or ill.

The power of attention and intention is enormous; although we may not realize it, it makes us the creators of our own fate. Yet the law of attraction is not an isolated law. It is just one of a complex pattern of many universal forces, which interact to ensure that we find fulfillment in life and achieve our goals. *The Secret* shows us just one important step on a path that leads much further, toward a more profound understanding of ourselves and the true purpose of our lives.

What *The Secret* does not acknowledge is our need to know ourselves before we can achieve our dreams. To create the life you want, you first need to investigate what it is that you use to create your reality. Most people continue to create unconsciously, from a place within themselves that they do not even know or are not willing to know. A place, above all, that is often filled with self-doubt, fears, resentment, negative thoughts, guilt, and pain. But the effects of your intentions are influenced by the purity of their source. Before unleashing your mental powers on the universe, you need to understand *why* you want what you want and where that desire comes from. Before we can use our powers of creation effectively, we must all get to the core of who we are.

The creators of *The Secret* know very well that most people are searching for a magical cure—ready-made solutions for complex problems—and that others focus mainly on their material desires: the sudden appearance of an ideal mate (or a new flat-screen television) sounds so much more attainable and attractive than gaining more insight into yourself and what your unique contribution to life could be.

Yet the real secret is hidden in the latter. Those who accumulate self-knowledge and become more loving, richer, and more liberated on an inner level have more to give. And those who have more to give will be amazed at what the universe has to give *them* and the secrets of life in which they will be able to share.

ANNEMARIE POSTMA

THE TWELVE LAWS
OF CREATION

We are all creating continually, whether we are conscious of it or not. In order to create the life that you were born to live, you must become aware of your creative power, harness it, and learn to use it purposefully. You are a direct reflection of the universe with its unlimited potential, and there is nothing you cannot achieve. But this is not the same as saying that you can bend the universe to your will.

The universe knows exactly what you want; it hears each and every one of your wishes and desires. But it also sees where your desires come from and whether or not they will serve you well. It knows your life purpose and can tell whether you are living in line with that purpose. The universe is intelligent, loving, and generous; it always gives you exactly what you require, but not always what you *think* you need.

The universe does not respond to displays of neediness. It loves powerful, authentic individuals with enough self-esteem and trust to enter into equal partnership with it. It wants to know if you have the courage to fully participate in your fate. Only then can the universe gather all its forces to help you fulfill your potential.

This book teaches you to work with the universe on all the important levels of your existence. It guides you to create the life you want, the life you were meant to live—not by fantasizing about having your every wish magically fulfilled, but by working with twelve powerful laws of creation, of which the law of attraction is only a small part. These laws combined form your real creative power.

Each of the chapters ahead explores the workings of one of the twelve laws and ends with a set of suggestions for putting it into practice in your own life. Many of these suggestions call for reflection and self-examination, which you can do in whatever way works best for you—perhaps by writing in a journal or meditating on key questions. There is a meditation practice at the end of the book that you may find useful as a method for your inner inquiries.

The Laws

Nothing just falls out of the sky, however much you wish for it and however positively you think. The real secret to getting what you want is threefold. The first step is to refine the quality of your wish so that you are clear about what you want and why, and you truly believe it can be yours. The second step involves an inner *decision* to want what you want with the whole of your heart and mind. The third step is taking full responsibility for your choice and its consequences.

WANTING

You can't really want something until no other option is attractive enough for you to devote your energy to. This point is different for everyone; some people are prepared to try a new path only when their backs are against the wall, when change is their last resort because their old, familiar ways of thinking and acting no longer bring the abundance they crave into their lives. The truth is, if you are still holding onto your old beliefs and making excuses for continuing in your old way of thinking and acting, then you don't *really* want it yet. The laws of creation ask you to take a hard look at your wants.

DECIDING

When you want something with your entire being, then you are ready to decide that you will do what you must to make sure that your desires become reality.

Are you ready to make that decision? Though it is an inner decision, it's not something vague or dreamy; on the contrary, it is concrete and can be made very practical, especially if you make it a sacred agreement with yourself. The laws of creation call for a thoughtful process of decision-making. What will your life look like if you make your decision a reality? What will it be like if you keep holding on to your old, limiting beliefs?

TAKING RESPONSIBILITY

When you are truly prepared to make your decision, you are also truly prepared to take full responsibility for all its consequences. The most important of these consequences is letting go of limiting beliefs on which a great deal of your existence has been built. Are you prepared to make your unconscious inner dialogue conscious if that's what it takes to free yourself from limiting beliefs? To do this, you will need to confront your deepest pain and fear, and the insecurities that lie hidden beneath your fear. Are you prepared to look within yourself when you come up against your limitations, when nothing seems to be going your way? The laws of creation require you to strip away, one by one, the limiting inner beliefs that prevent you from making free choices and creating the life of your dreams.

Wanting

Law 1

RELEASE YOUR WILL

There are many paths in life,

but of all these paths

There is one that you must travel.

That path and that one alone is for you.

And whether you want to or not,

you must travel that path.

So the choice is not the path, because it chose you.

The choice is how you travel that path.

With unwillingness for the pitfalls and the stones,

With resistance because the sun is barely able to reach

a path that cuts through ravines.

Or with the will to be gentler and

wiser at the end of that path

than you were at the beginning.

The path chose you: will you choose it too?

HANS STOLP

"It's simple. You are living if you're breathing and your heart is beating," says a good friend of mine who is always able to explain complicated matters in a very straightforward way. "After that you fill life in. It's no more difficult than that."

Often we are busier with "filling in" life than we are with living it. Like fish, we gasp for air as we go along. And we take our heartbeats for granted. That is how it has to be, because we are busy. Busy with filling in, wishing, dreaming, planning, and especially . . . wanting. Wanting, wanting, wanting. We want so much, though we are not always aware of why we want what we want, or even exactly what it is we want. Our will drives our existence. And with that will we keep ourselves going, we create the path on which we walk.

◉

A strong will can help you face
the obstacles in your life, but sometimes things simply
unfold by themselves.

◉

I believe in the power of will. My willpower has brought me a long way in my life. When, as an eleven-year-old girl, I suddenly ended up in a wheelchair as a paraplegic, my will was the instrument for winning back my place in ordinary life. When my mother died at an early age, I exercised my *will* in order to experience her death as meaningful. During periods when I became seriously ill, it was my will that allowed me to survive. And in my work my will was also the means for successfully traveling what seemed like impossible paths. I set my goals, went for them completely, and achieved them. I became the first professional model in Europe in a wheelchair, built a career as a successful columnist and publicist, and wrote many books about self-esteem that have since become bestsellers.

●

Sometimes not getting what you want
is the best thing
that can happen to you.

●

But over the years my views on the manipulability of existence on the strength of sheer willpower have changed. Although it is true that a strong will can help you to face the obstacles in your life, sometimes your will is unnecessary and things simply unfold. That insight came as a result of trial and error. There many moments in my life in which everything went differently to the way I had wanted, or in which I was unexpectedly confronted with despair and pain. And after the mist of disappointment, anger, or frustration had finally lifted, I always thought afterwards: how fortunate that life did not give me what I wanted. Because later on I always saw that something knew what I needed for my development far better than I did. Sometimes, not getting what you want is the best thing that can happen to you.

❖

You often think that you know what is good for you.
But what is good for you is usually what is taking place
at that moment.

❖

Recently, I took a very old book out of the bookcase, *The Wisdom and Beauty of China* by Henri Borel. A chapter entitled "Wu Wei" contains this lovely passage:

Do you not know how the Yellow Emperor found his magic pearl again? I will tell you. The Yellow Emperor traveled to the north of the Red Lake and ascended the tops of the K'un-Lun Mountains. Returning south he lost his magic pearl. He employed Intelligence to find it, but without success. He employed Magic to find it, but without success. He employed Extreme Power to find it, but without success. Finally, he employed Nothing and Nothing got it. "How strange!" cried the Yellow Emperor, "that Nothing was able to get it! Do you understand me, young man?"

The chapter "Wu Wei" beautifully emphasizes the power of "action through inaction": a force that we often overlook because we think that we can direct and control everything. It reminds us that there are two ways of wanting: the way of grasping and the way of letting go.

Willpower is excellent fuel for surviving. But in order to learn how to *live* and to receive the real abundance of the universe, we need more advanced inner tools, tools like self-knowledge, courage, surrender, and trust. Most people find it easy to let go of things that are not very dear to them; they allow the universe or God to handle that part. If something is very important, we try to solve it ourselves. At the same time, we notice that when we do let go of what is most important to us, the universe takes care of things well.

Will helps us part of the way. But at the end of the path you can "achieve" lies a path that you must simply travel: an unknown path with no reassurance or guarantees. A path beyond the will, yet one that is your true path. And it is here that one of the keys to The Deeper Secret can be found: instead of imposing your will on reality to get what you want, learn to want what appears. You often think that you know what is good for you. But what is good for you is usually what is taking place at that moment. By resisting the path that lies ahead for you, you may miss the universe's real messages.

•

Will helps us part of the way.
But at the end of the path you can "achieve" lies a path
that you must simply travel.

•

Recently, I saw a talk show that featured *The Secret*. A very disappointed woman was sitting in the audience. "I was a fan from the first minute this book came out," she told the talk-show host. "I even started to hold workshops about it with my sister. But after a year of doing this, I have to acknowledge that the theory doesn't work." The host asked her how she had arrived at this conclusion. "Well, because I've been thinking positively for a year now and visualized certain things strongly, but I still haven't got what I wanted, like a house in the country, on the edge of a forest, for example. I did actually move like I wanted, but now I live in a suburb full of concrete!"

❦

You don't get what you want; you get what you need for your inner growth.

❦

Her disillusionment points up a major misconception about *The Secret*. Many people read the book, watch the DVD, and then get frustrated when they do not get what they want. "Why does everything always go wrong, even when I use *The Secret*?" they ask. The answer to this is very simple: you do not get what you want; you get what you *need* for your inner growth. You act like a magnet, drawing people and experiences to you that resonate with how you think about yourself and what you wish for yourself. You attract exactly that which agrees with your unconscious needs, desires, doubts, and fears.

It also works the other way around; you do not attract anything you are not ready for or anything you cannot fully allow yourself to have. That is why it is important to know when to let go of your will. At the moment you notice that you are being sent in another direction—that you are meeting resistance and what you have wished for is not appearing—it is not the Law of Attraction that is at work, but what I call the *Law of Redirection*. When you are pursuing goals for yourself that no longer give you what you need for your growth, the Law of Redirection steps in. It works on the principle of repulsion rather than attraction, repelling things that do not serve you and, conversely, attracting things that allow you to see clearly that you are no longer on the right path. In these moments, let go of your will, surrender, and wait. Calmly look to see where the Law of Redirection is trying to send you. That is the true direction that is destined for you at this moment. If you keep on putting your willpower into the old path, then the Law of Redirection will continue to step in, and it will show you more and more clearly that the path you are following is no longer yours.

Summary

- The universe does not give you what you want, it gives you what you *need* for your inner growth.

- You act like a magnet to draw people and experiences to yourself that resonate with how you think about yourself, what you wish for yourself, and what you think you are worth.

- You attract that which agrees with your unconscious needs, desires, doubts, and fears.

- You often think that you know best what is good for you —but what is good for you is usually just what is actually taking place at that moment. A key to The Deeper Secret is to learn to want what appears.

- By fighting reality and resisting the path that lies ahead for you, you often miss the universe's real messages.

- Whenever you notice that you are being turned aside from your goal, it is not the Law of Attraction that is at work, but the *Law of Redirection*.

- The universe uses resistance to show you that you are no longer on the right path and that you should let go of the reins of your will.

Affirmation

I have used my energy, power, and love to manifest my desires as far as possible, and now I let go. I have faith that things are as they should be, because the entire universe is as it should be. Everything that unfolds is right for me and my path in this life.

In Practice

- Use your will gratefully as an instrument of creation, but do not impose it on anything if you experience resistance.

- Remember that there are two ways of wanting: grasping and letting go. When the grasping will does not bring you the health, love, happiness, and success you want, let go of your will and hand over the reins to the universe.

- Ask yourself if you are using your will to try to change your path. Try instead to accept whatever appears on your path and see it as a pointer for your inner growth.

- Promise yourself that you will step in if the energy of your will threatens to take over your life again. Do not rebuke yourself in these moments; instead, consciously do something else to "ground" yourself. Go for a walk in the forest or on the beach, prepare a healthy meal for your loved ones, or take a lovely bath with relaxing essential oils.

- Realize that you do not need to change yourself into someone you think you ought to be. You do not have to go anywhere, do anything, or be anyone other than exactly who you are now.

Law 2

WANT WITH
YOUR HEART

The mind can warn us what we should avoid.
The heart can tell us what we should do.

JOSEPH JOUBERT

*W*hen I entered the ordinary world again as a sixteen-year-old after a rehabilitation period of many years, my father used to say: "Whatever you do, make sure that later on you go to university, because it's important in view of your disability." Obviously, there was a hint of truth in this. Knowledge seemed likely to increase anyone's chance of a "successful life," mine included. So after receiving my secondary-school diploma, I went to study law in Amsterdam. Once I'd completed my degree, I promised myself, I'd be free to do as I pleased.

Despite this, not only did I almost fall asleep every time I sat in the lecture hall, but something always went wrong when I made a genuine effort to apply myself. For instance, months passed and I was still having trouble finding the right classroom. If I did manage to find it, then I couldn't get in because I was late and the door had already been locked. And every day when I drove to school in my car, I had the feeling that I was driving in the wrong direction.

Looking back, these were all wonderfully symbolic "roadblocks" that discouraged me every day from continuing to stumble along the wrong path for too long. After eighteen months I gave up my law studies and went on to do other things. I took a course on presentation and interview techniques for television, a camera acting class, and two marketing courses, then I decided I would like to do some modeling work. My father, who had owned an advertising agency for years and knew what was in store for me, would look worried. "Sweetheart," he used to say, "the path you're choosing is extremely tough, even if you aren't in a wheelchair." But however well-meaning, loving, and right those warnings may have been, whenever I followed my heart, lots of things seemed to just work out and "happen" by themselves.

●

As long as we create walls
in our thinking and our beliefs,
we will continue to be trapped behind them.

●

The direction I chose was one that probably seemed completely illogical and unattainable to onlookers. For me it was simply the path I had to take; I followed the voice of my heart. Not that I was conscious of doing so at the time. I was simply conscious of the feeling that drew me in that direction, so strong that others' *ifs* and *buts* came across as totally unreal. I had a need to show the world, through my actions, that limitations exist primarily in our thoughts and that as long as we create walls in our thinking and our beliefs, we will continue to be trapped behind them. What I wanted to do felt like a mission.

●

As a child, I already had
a very deep belief in my possibilities.
This had nothing to do with unrealistic "dreams."
It was a profound trust and knowing:
this is how it will be.

●

Pondering my future had nothing to do with fantasizing about a magical "someday." As a child, I already had a very deep belief in my possibilities. This had nothing to do with unrealistic "dreams." It was a profound trust and knowing: this is how it will be. I had a powerful imagination, and from an early age I knew instinctively that thinking about something, being able to imagine it, was the first step in making it a reality. I became, as far as I know, the only professional photo model in Europe with a disability, and as a result I was a sought-after international television guest. In 1994, I made it to the Dutch semifinals of "The Look of the Year," a modeling competition organized by the prestigious model agency Elite. In 1995, my photo series was featured in *Playboy*, and that same year I wrote my first book, *I Love Me*, which immediately became a bestseller and is still selling well after many years.

I did things because my heart, not my mind, prompted me. What's more, everything that I achieved came about through loving working relationships with people who believed in me and had the same intention: to show that life becomes much more beautiful and exciting if you think in terms of possibilities instead of limitations, and that you can change your life if you demolish the barriers in your thinking and become aware of the lens through which you view your world.

●

Intention is
the ultimate creative power.
The law of creation starts with intention.

●

Intention means consciously creating by focusing your thoughts in the direction your feelings dictate. The law of creation *starts* with intention. Intention is the motor; making up your mind in this way is a necessary condition for creation. It is the ultimate creative power. Many people believe that you can create what you visualize. But visualization is only a tool, not the source of creativity. In the same way, the will and the ego are tools: they are the servants of intention, not the other way around. The will is a powerful instrument for creation, and there is nothing wrong with using that power. But the will must be guided by intention—the mind must be driven by the heart.

Intention is an expression of surrender, trust, and inner "knowing." An intention may not be specifically defined; in the past, I never thought, "I'm going to become a model" or "I'm going to write bestsellers about self-esteem and self-respect." As a little girl, I knew only that I wanted to contribute something to people's awareness, to show them a different, less limited way of looking at themselves and life. Ultimately, I put my will and my mind behind that intention, in that order. The important thing is to use your heart to decide what you want, then use your mind to empower your will and put it to work in the world. The will is not there to decide, it is there to receive and enact what has already been decided. That is how the law of creation works.

●

The important thing is to use your heart to decide what you want, then use your mind to empower your will and put it to work in the world.
That is how the law of creation works.

●

The power of intention is incredibly creative and immense. But forming an intention does not mean that you can sit back and let the universe do the rest. Quite the contrary. Being true to your intentions requires you to dedicate your entire being to them, investing them with all your energy—not the energy of the will, but the energy of the heart. This is the energy that is released when you let go of thinking and trust that whatever needs to be done—through the use of your will—will become clear to you. If your intention is pure and connected to your life's purpose, then unprecedented power will flow from the universe! Your perceptions will become more sensitive and all your senses will become sharper. As a result, you will experience more and more synchronicity, or meaningful coincidences, to speed your progress on your path.

●

There are two kinds of intention:
ego intention and heart intention.

●

There are two kinds of intention: ego intention and heart intention. Both have strong creative power, but their outcomes are completely different. Ego intention consists of fear, limitation, grasping, and control. Heart intention consists of love, freedom, surrender, and trust. Creating from ego intention brings forth more ego; creating from heart intention brings forth more heart. The choice is yours!

Every day, around the world, an enormous amount of creation takes place through ego intention. But ego can never create more than itself; it cannot create beyond the bounds of what it knows. And the ego wants only one thing: its own security. The ego wants to know what is going to happen in life; it wants to make plans and to see into the future, to anticipate life's surprises. It wants to define life, to speed it up or slow it down. That is why the ego thinks that to acquire power, status, and wealth is paramount to existence. This is how it creates the illusion that it has control over life.

●

However positive ego intention may seem,
it is always rooted in fear.

●

With ego intention, everything revolves around you, your happiness, your well-being, and your success. It doesn't matter how positive the actions it prompts may seem, it is always rooted in fear. So much of what we do is motivated by fear—of lack, of inadequacy, of losing control. If you suffer from a lack of self-esteem and genuine self-confidence, you will always need to prove something to the outside world.

●

So much of what we do is motivated by fear—fear of lack, of inadequacy, of losing control.

●

If your intention arises from your ego, then you will undoubtedly be able to achieve a great deal. The more you feel you need to prove something to the outside world— or to yourself—the more you will strengthen your intention to get what you need. But an intention that is based on the ego is ultimately limiting, characterized, ironically, by the ego's limitless, insatiable depth. Nothing will ever be enough to satisfy the ego's hunger. And as long as you are investing your actions with that energy, the universe cannot lead you in the ways of the heart. Even the most positive things that you can achieve with ego intention can never reach further than the boundaries of self-interest.

❦

Heart intention leads to
action that arises from your deepest being.

❦

Heart intention is something completely different. Heart intention is noble; it does not arise from a selfish need for confirmation and appreciation. Heart intention is not driven primarily by money, power, status, or fame, but is based instead on love, trust, and truth. Heart intention leads to action that arises from your deepest being. It is "guided action": you do the right thing at exactly the right moment, even if the right thing is to do nothing at all. Heart intention allows you to act from your inner self and at the same time as part of a greater plan.

❦

When you strive for truth in your life, the universe will
encourage you by giving you a sign: stillness.

❦

Acting with heart intention does not prevent you from acquiring money, power, status, wealth, and fame, but these are not the goals; they are the results of the life that you have chosen to live. If you live from heart intention, you live from a higher level of consciousness, and you feel connected to all life. Your intentions are an expression of your love, compassion, and goodness. You love yourself so that you can love others. You take good care of yourself so that you can also take care of others. You accumulate in order to share. Your money, power, success, status, and fame are your tools. You enjoy your achievements because they open doors for you so that you can be of even greater service to the world.

How can you be certain where *your* intention arises? After all, the ego is a master of illusion. But if you are living from the heart, striving for truth in your life, the universe will encourage you in this by giving you a sign: stillness. If you are striving mainly for your own well-being, you'll get a different sign: discouragement and restlessness.

When you live from heart intention, the universe can

conspire to serve you more easily. After all, it is safer to burden someone with all the riches of life if you know that he will not use this wealth to glorify his ego and himself, but will handle it responsibly. And because your goal is not to earn money or acquire power or status, if these things are given to you, you will not fear them. Instead, you can enjoy them to the full and value them—without becoming attached to them and fearful of losing them. You are the one who possesses money—it will not possess you. You are the one who uses power—that power will not misuse you. And you will devote yourself to doing good—not define yourself by doing it. You are given the things to which you do not attach your ego; that is the universal law. When you free yourself of neediness, you are ready to receive; that is the great secret.

●

You are given the things to which you do not attach your ego; that is the universal law. When you free yourself of neediness, you are ready to receive; that is the great secret.

●

HEART INTENTION	EGO INTENTION
Love	*Fear*
Faith	*Mistrust*
Love of truth	*Need for well-being*
Generous	*Narrow-minded*
Abundance	*Lack*
Free	*Needy*
Non-attached	*Attached*
Freedom	*Limitation*
Stillness	*Restlessness*
Giving	*Taking*
Flexible	*Rigid*
Open	*Closed*
Developing peace	*Controlling through violence*
Self-conquest	*Self-defense*
Service	*Self-interest*
Working anonymously	*Chasing fame*
Looking for solutions	*Fighting problems*

Summary

- The law of creation *begins* with intention, which means focusing your thoughts in the way your feelings dictate.

- You use your heart to decide what you want, then use your mind to empower your will and bring about what you want. That is how the law of creation works.

- There are two kinds of intention: ego intention and heart intention. Ego intention consists of fear, limitation, grasping, and control. Heart intention consists of love, freedom, surrender, and trust.

- With ego intention everything revolves around you, your happiness, your well-being, and your success.

- Heart intention is not primarily driven by money, power, status, or fame; if you receive these, they are simply the results of the way you've chosen to live.

- When you live from heart intention, the universe can conspire to serve you more easily.

- You are given the things to which you do not attach your ego; that is the universal law.

Affirmation

I am a center of intention. I find abundance in my alignment with the universe and I learn to direct my intentions and make them reality. I live from my heart to manifest my spiritual purpose.

In Practice

- Think about whether you are living from trust or mistrust. Which one better describes your underlying attitude toward life?

- Ask yourself these questions: What are my motives for taking action or letting things be? Why am I alive? Do I live from a love of truth, in order to get to know life? Or do I live from a need for well-being, primarily concerned with seeking out pleasant experiences and improving my personal circumstances?

- You know now that the universe gives you signs that discourage you from seeking merely your own well-being and encourage you to strive for truth. What signs are you being given: dissatisfaction and restlessness or stillness and peace?

- For everything that you encounter on your path, always consciously ask yourself: How do I react? Do I allow myself to be encouraged or discouraged to follow my heart intention? Do I open my heart further or do I close myself off?

Law 3

KNOW WHY YOU
WANT WHAT
YOU WANT

I should have been
more specific.

MARGARET CHO

The Korean-American stand-up comic Margaret Cho once said in one of her shows, "From the time I was a little girl I wished that I would be surrounded by beautiful men when I grew up. And I got what I wanted: my life was jam-packed with gorgeous men. They're all gay. I should have been more specific."

If you want something, it is important to know why you want it and to be specific about what it is that you want. If you want something without knowing why, you can't be specific when you make your wish. And if you aren't specific, your wish is incomplete. For example, if you go shopping without knowing exactly what, you want, you can spend hours browsing, but you come home with nothing.

●

When you want something
without knowing why, your wish is incomplete.

●

If, like the woman on the talk show in the first chapter, you want a house in the country, you need to ask yourself, *Why do I want to live in the country?* And if, for example, the answer to this question is *Because I have a need for inner peace*, then your real wish is for inner peace. You assume that a house in the country will bring you that inner peace, so you come to believe that the house itself is the object of your desire.

Perhaps the thing you really want—in this case, inner peace—is available to you in other ways. But because you aren't connected to your real wish, you don't recognize what the universe already gives you or the various forms in which it presents itself. If you don't know why you want what you want, you won't know it when you see it. This is the reason why so many people think that *The Secret* doesn't work for them, when in fact it works all the time.

●

If you don't know why you want what you want, you won't know it when you see it.

●

For example, *The Secret* says: Do you want a new car? Then you'll get a new car. *The Deeper Secret* says: ask yourself what the underlying energy of the wish is—what need do you think the car is going to fulfill? Manifestation follows feeling, not the other way around. That's why it's important to feel what you want in order to allow *The Secret* to work.

Imagine that you actually are looking for a new house. Don't focus on the size of the house, its style, or its details. Focus on how you'll feel when that house is as you would like it to be. Wish with your heart. Later, when you find the house that turns out to be right for you, you'll be able to recognize the house as your house because of how it feels. At that moment, you'll say, "Hey, I feel the same feeling that I expected my 'ideal house' to give me."

•

The Secret says, do you want a new car? Then you'll get a new car. The Deeper Secret asks, what need do you think the car is going to fulfill?

•

As another example, imagine that I were to wish that I could walk again. I would then need to consider, why do I want to walk? And suppose the answer to this is, *I want to walk because I want to be more independent than I am now.* I then need to ask myself, why do I want to be independent? *So I can be free.* Why do I want to be free? *So I can more easily reach my potential in this lifetime; because I need to be free to create.* Why do I want to create? *Because that's why I'm alive.* I'm alive to gain insight into the mechanics of self-esteem and self-respect and the effects they have on our lives, other people, the environment, and the animal kingdom. If that is my goal, I need a platform. Perhaps I believe that if I can walk, I will be able to create my platform more easily. Which brings me full circle. Why do I want to walk? Because I don't think I can be happy if I can't walk. And there's my real wish. I want to be happy!

●

Imagine that I were to wish that I could walk again. The question would then be: why do I want to walk?

●

There's only one way to communicate with the universe and that's by using your feelings. The universe is energy, so it can only help you energetically. It works with form, but it doesn't understand the language of form. This means that you need to transform the goal you are seeking help with into energy so that the universe can understand it. If you wish for a new house, the universe can't bring you a new house. But if you communicate the feeling you want that new house to give you, the universe can help you—very easily, in fact.

Would you like a new job? Ask yourself how you want to feel in that job. Maybe you want authority and the right to make decisions. So you pick up a newspaper or a professional journal and decide to select jobs based only on the feeling you get from the job description, instead of looking at the education or experience required to do that job. Once you've chosen a listing this way, ask yourself: what's standing in the way of me getting this job? Ask yourself if you have the skills it calls for, and if you don't, find a way to acquire them, such as by taking a course.

This is how the law of creation works, not the other way around. It is not true that you can spend a year visualizing a job as director of a successful multinational and then have it land in your lap, even though you have no relevant experience or college degree. But if you wish for something, you can really wish from the depths of your being, and then the entire universe will conspire to help you.

●

The universe is energy, so it can only help energetically.
It works with form, but it doesn't understand
the language of form.

●

Be Specific

If you want to work with the universe, you need to be specific. Know what you want and why you want what you want. Only then can you recognize the miracles that the universe puts in your path in order to fulfill your wish.

Meditate on whatever it is you wish for: the right house, the new job, the perfect love. Visualize yourself having it, and focus on the feeling it gives you. That's the feeling you are striving for. That feeling usually manifests itself differently than your ego expects. Be ready to recognize it in whatever form it presents itself.

Summary

- When you want something, it is important to be specific about what you want and to know why you want it.

- If you don't know what you want or why you want it, you may not recognize the various forms it appears in when the universe grants your wish.

- There's only one way to communicate with the universe and that's by using your feelings. The universe doesn't understand the language of form. The universe is energy, so it can only receive requests in the language of energy.

- To make your desire understandable to the universe, you need to translate the goal you are striving for into the language of energy. If you wish for a new house, the universe can't bring you a new house. But if you communicate the feeling you want that new house to give you, then the universe can help you easily.

Affirmation

---

*I let go of attachment to the forms in which my desires
appear. I know what I want from deep within,
and I trust in that feeling. I recognize that my
wish will be manifested in the way that the universe
considers right for me.*

In Practice

- To translate each material goal into the language of energy, look closely at what you want, and always ask why. Why do you want that job, that relationship, that other house, and so on? If it's because you want more responsibility, more romance, or more living space, why do you want those things? What feeling are you striving for? Go as many steps as it takes to reach your heart's deepest desire.

- Try to remember the dreams and wishes of your childhood. What feelings did those wishes give you? What kind of life did you think they would help you create for yourself?

- Ask yourself, peacefully and in silence: *What is it that I really want, what do I want to do with my life? What do I want to receive, what do I want to be able to give? Which wishes are most alive within me?*

- Putting aside considerations of the outside world and your own circumstances, ask yourself: *What would I like to give to others, what do I want to contribute to the world, and what do I want to leave behind when I'm no longer here?*

Law 4

BELIEVE IN WHAT YOU WANT

Whatever you believe
you experience.

EVA PIERRAKOS

*K*nowing what you want doesn't necessarily mean that you believe it can be achieved. But believing is the difference between failure and success. Limiting beliefs form the main stumbling block on the path to actually achieving what you want. If you believe, and if you are prepared to use all the energy and resources that the universe makes available to you, then failure is not an option.

I saw a lovely example of this in top tennis player Serena Williams at the beginning of 2007, during the Australian Open. When she came onto the court and I saw the look in her eyes, I thought, there's no way this girl can lose this match. At the time she was out of shape, twenty pounds too heavy, and it was her first major competition after coming back from an injury, and she was playing against a super-fit Russian. During the match, she got a cramp, and at one point it literally seemed that she could not run. She was on the verge of losing. The clouds were gathering and it was threatening to rain. Serena stumbled across the court and looked hopefully into the sky, surely praying that the rain would come and give her a reprieve. She had already taken time out for medical treatment, and you're only entitled to one treatment during each competition.

Suddenly it started pouring, and Serena's body was given the recovery time she had asked for. The universe had seen the look in her eye, which did not show a single doubt; she was going to win this competition, no matter how. So if it meant taking advantage of the rain when her body couldn't stand any more, then she would take it. Her belief in her own ability was completely untinged by doubt. And she won. Not only the quarterfinals, but the semifinals and the final too, something that no one had expected.

●

If you don't believe in what you want, you will not be able to receive it. In order to believe, you need the courage to risk undesirable answers and outcomes, and the desire to know the truth with heart and soul.

●

Now you begin to see how the universe operates. This powerfully dazzling sea of energy can manifest anything you can think of, from ultimate abundance and bliss to extreme scarcity, and everything in between. This realization can change your life at a very deep level. You live in a pliable substance to which your beliefs give shape. If there is just one percent of doubt in what you wish for, your wish will not be manifested.

The universe doesn't hear what you wish for; it feels it. Deep belief is something you feel, which is why it is the first step towards creating. It sets a powerful creative force in motion with which you give the universe the tools to support you. If you really believe that you can change, that you can grow beyond negativity, destructiveness, fear, inadequacy, and despair, and that the universe is nothing but abundance, then you must and will experience this.

On the other hand, if you believe that your life cannot be changed, that the universe is badly predisposed towards you and holds nothing good for you, then you must and will experience precisely that, because all your thoughts, deeds, and feelings will be focused on the negative. You'll create a self-fulfilling prophecy, and when you don't get what you wish for, you will say, "See, I knew it."

If you don't believe in what you want, you will not be able to receive it. An intention, after all, is essentially an expression of belief. Believing is the first step; it sets energy in motion. When you want without believing, you are no longer dynamically participating in your life, you're just waiting until the universe gives you a sign that the coast is clear. Many people live this way. They want certainty. They are not prepared to believe until they know roughly what the outcome will be if they believe. But that's not how it works; that is not faith.

Faith requires action instead of reaction. It calls for initiative and daring rather than anxious, fearful expectation. To have real faith, you must have the willingness to tackle any obstacles in your path, the courage to risk undesirable answers and outcomes, and the desire to know the truth with heart and soul. You arrive at real faith only by truly opening yourself to reality. Anything less merely gives the illusion of faith.

*

Most people want certainty.
They are not prepared to believe until they know roughly
what the outcome will be if they do.

*

Faith is not something that you cling to in spite of experience; in fact, believing and experiencing are closely linked. If I were booked to give a lecture about the laws of creation and didn't believe I could do it, then I would call the organizer and cancel. But instead of doing this, I ask myself: how can I add value to the afternoon for these people? And I wholeheartedly believe I can, so I go ahead with it. I use my faith to create an experience. It also works the other way around: you develop faith through experience, from the results of your actions. Athletes are a good examples of this; their belief in themselves arises and grows as a result of action. If you want to jump over a wide ditch, you may not accomplish it until your tenth attempt, but by keeping at it you gain faith in your own ability.

Experience and courage lie between knowing and believing. To "know" something is not at all the same as to believe it in your heart. How many self-help books have you read lately? And how many of these books made you think, *I already know all this, it's nothing new to me?* But how often have you acted on these things you already know? Not so often, you say? Why not? You know that the things you read are true, but you don't believe that it pays to put them into practice. For example, you may say you *know* that if you let go and trust, you will receive everything you need for your path in life. But you don't *believe* it, so you're afraid to take the risk. Instead, you wait for the universe to take the first step and show you that, if you let go and trust, the reward that you expect really will follow!

*

*Experience and courage
lie between knowing and believing.*

*

Faith asks something else of you as well. It requires you to believe that what you wish for is actually right for you, and that you yourself have the potential to attain your desire. I have never met anyone whose wishes were unrealistic or unattainable, no matter how distant their goals seemed from their current circumstances. And it is no coincidence that certain wishes are held by certain people. It seems to me that the wish chooses the person who is best able to carry it out.

Take my best friend, Monique. She dreamed of being a star athlete and coach and as she grew up she played tennis and water polo, and was extremely good at horseback riding and sailing. But she excelled at hockey. Then, when she was fourteen, a malignant tumor in her back paralyzed her from the waist down, putting an end to her dream.

What is faith?

Many spiritual traditions use the word *faith* to describe a
state of positive acceptance that makes it possible to enter
and embrace reality with an open heart and without fear.
When I use the word, I'm not talking about unquestion-
ingly accepting religious dogma or things that cannot
be proven scientifically. For me, above all, faith means
believing in the logic, love, and goodness of the universe.
Faith enables us to look at life as beautiful, even when
it is not beautiful. It allows us to trust in the way things
happen, however confounding or painful those things
sometimes are. Having genuine faith means being truly
prepared for things not to go as you hope or expect, being
prepared to meet everything in life and within yourself.
It means trusting that things are as they should be, even
when they are not as you would like them to be, because
the entire universe is as it should be.

●

It is no coincidence that certain wishes are held by certain people. It seems to me that the wish chooses the person who is best able to carry it out.

●

But Monique had an unshakeable faith in herself, and she firmly intended to continue her sports career. In 1984 she became a Paralympic table tennis champion, and in 1986 she made the transition to wheelchair tennis. Between 1992 and 1996 she won three Paralympic gold medals and four world titles in wheelchair tennis, which made her the world's first Paralympic champion in two different individual sports. She was a pioneer in the field of wheelchair tennis and paved the way for the many handicapped players who followed her. In addition to all this, Monique built a highly successful international career in the business world. She married her tennis coach, and, though she was thought to be infertile as a result of the chemotherapy in her youth, they had a perfectly healthy son. In the eyes of the world, Monique's ambitions and desires might well have seemed unattainable, yet she showed that there is no such thing as a truly impossible dream.

Time and again I find that a person's wishes are perfectly aligned with that person and his or her life path. Monique wished what she needed to wish, believed in what she wanted and did what she needed to do to make it a reality. Because she did so, she is now the role model that she was destined to be in this life, using the unique intersection of her talent, her disability, and her desire to inspire others to connect with their inner power and to truly believe in what they want.

●

Time and again I find that a person's wishes are perfectly aligned with that person and his or her life path.

●

Do you believe in what you want?

YOU: I want to be happy.

THE UNIVERSE: But do you believe you can be happy?

YOU: Not really.

THE UNIVERSE: Having faith in the way I work has everything to do with having faith in yourself. If you don't believe that you can be happy, then how can I help you?

You won't be able to recognize anything I give you and you'll never be able to receive it openly.

YOU: But I can't believe something until I've seen it. How can I let go and trust unless I know how things will turn out?

THE UNIVERSE: I follow your faith, and faith means being willing to face whatever comes. *You* set it in motion. I only work to help you once you have taken the first step.

Summary

- Limiting beliefs form the number one stumbling block in achieving what you want.

- If there is one percent of doubt in what you want, then your desire will not manifest.

- If you really believe that you can change, that you can grow beyond negativity, fear, inadequacy, and hopelessness, and that the universe holds nothing but abundance—even for you—then you must and will experience this.

- If you believe that your life cannot be changed, that the universe is badly disposed towards you, and that nothing but a negative fate awaits you, you will experience precisely that.

- Faith calls for action instead of reaction; it requires initiative, daring, and the willingness to experience.

- Real faith can only come if you are not tense and fearful, but prepared to deal with all that comes into your path, whatever that may be.

- Having faith requires the courage to risk undesirable answers and outcomes, the readiness to overcome obstacles, and the desire to know the truth with heart and soul.

Affirmation

---

*I believe in myself and my possibilties and
I have faith in the future. I trust in things as they are
and in myself as I am.*

In Practice

- Resolve to find out which obstacles, limiting beliefs, and fears, conscious or unconscious, undermine your faith and trust. To help you with your inquiry, you might start by reading a good book on self-esteem or, if you like, investigate different forms of professional guidance.

- Start a journal and write down every day how often you think negatively about yourself and your possibilities, about others, and about life. Resolve to keep this daily record for seven weeks, because seven is the spiritual number of change, associated with truth, love for yourself, and inner growth. (It also takes about seven weeks to form a new habit!)

- During this time, also note how often you take part in conversations that include gossiping, complaining about illness or misfortune, or discussing how complicated and difficult life is. This will help you recognize and acknowledge negativity in yourself, a prerequisite for learning to be positive and to believe in yourself and others.

- For these seven weeks, resolve to lovingly embrace everything that you would normally be afraid of, feel resistance to, or want to run away from. Welcome everything that appears on your path in the next seven weeks without any judgement at all.

- For these seven weeks, assume that the universe's logical, positive, and loving intentions are at work in every event and encounter on your path.

Deciding

Law 5

MAKE A DECISION,
MAKE A CHOICE

Nothing will happen
unless you make a decision.

OPRAH WINFREY

*T*o get what you want, you have to be conscious of what you want and why, and to believe that it can be yours. But "wanting," by itself, is meaningless. We can spend all day "wanting" to escape from it all, without taking a single step toward any outcome. "Wanting" lacks the crucial element of decision.

I speak to people every day who want all kinds of things—to write a book, lose weight, travel to Nepal, have a fulfilling relationship, or simply be happy. If you say, "I want to be happy," you aren't really saying anything. Yes, you're saying that you want to be happy—but you cannot be happy until you *decide* to be happy. This is a trap many people fall into: they think they already know what they want, so there's nothing wrong with their motivation and nothing more is required. But you can only become happy when you pluck up the courage to really stand up for your decision.

Making a decision is an act of will. It requires that you uncover your thought patterns—however negative and painful they may be—and get to know them, then release them from a place of total acceptance. Making a decision means daring to set goals, focusing your energy, and taking full responsibility for all the consequences of what you wish for. Obviously, "wanting" is much safer! As soon as you really decide to "want" something, you are committed to realizing your wish.

●

Making a decision means daring to set goals, focusing your energy, and taking full responsibility for all the consequences of what you wish for.

●

There are always things in life that we cannot control or direct. Some things just happen, inviting us to arrive at acceptance and surrender. Yet many things hinge on taking a decision and making a choice. Take love, for example: we all *want* love. But love doesn't just drop out of the sky. If you *decide* you want to experience true love, you must first turn the searchlight on yourself and do the inner work that it requires. This is because you will never find anything outside yourself that is not already present on the inside, and you can't receive anything from someone else that you aren't able to give yourself.

Love is a good example of the active decision that wanting requires. Falling in love is chemical; it is something that happens to us. Falling in love doesn't require effort or strain. On the other hand, loving another person is an *act of will* that usually far transcends pleasurable feelings of attachment. Love is not just something you feel; it is something you do. It calls for the willingness to face our fears, to let go of control, to open ourselves to the unknown, and to embrace our obligation to learn. Love asks that before exercising our will, we first put aside our neediness. Love requires the courage and the ability to face our own fears and to go beyond the boundaries of our ego. To truly love is a decision of the most active and accountable kind.

How will you decide?

ARE YOU FACED WITH A DIFFICULT DECISION?
THEN ASK YOURSELF THE FOLLOWING
QUESTIONS:

1. What are my choices here?

2. What are my excuses for not deciding?

3. Which consequences of my decision am I afraid of?

4. Why am I afraid of these consequences?

5. Do I usually make decisions myself, or do I wait until the decision is made for me?

6. Do I make decisions at the right time?

7. Do I know which decisions are truly important for me?

8. Am I able to trust my intuition when making decisions?

9. Are my decisions based on faith in myself and my possibilities?

Remember, indecision is creative energy too, only it creates without direction or focus.

Happiness and success, too, are questions of choice. The secret of those who are sincerely happy and successful is that they are able to do one thing: make decisions. In most situations, the first thing you need to do is to make a decision—*really* make one. I once saw someone walking around wearing a T-shirt that said, "If you refuse to choose you lose." A decision by definition involves a choice. Unfortunately, many people do refuse to choose. As a result, they don't achieve what they want or get what they wish for, because if you don't decide in life, life decides for you.

At first glance, many people seem to be deciding and choosing. In reality, unconsciously they are doing nothing more than anticipating and reacting. There's a big difference. When you decide to participate in your fate, you send out active energy. When you react, you send out passive energy, and it is hard for the universe to help you. You will have difficulty in recognizing that everything it puts in your path is a product of your creative power, since you have not yet confirmed your desire with any decision. You haven't accepted that you are creating in the first place, so you don't do anything with what you create. But remember, indecision is creative energy too, only it creates without direction or focus.

A Sacred Pledge

To see what it takes to act on what you decide, make a decision about something important to you, and consider it a sacred pledge you make to yourself. Take a sheet of paper and write your decision at the top of the page. Below, write down the limiting beliefs you will need to let go of to make your wish a reality. Then divide the rest of the paper into two columns. In the left-hand column, write down in more detail what you have decided, why you have decided this, and why the decision is so important to you. Underneath, write down how your life will look if you make this decision a reality. In the right-hand column, write down how your life will look if you don't make this decision, but continue to hold on to your old, limiting beliefs. Put this paper in your journal, then look at it every Friday evening to see if your thoughts, choices, and actions during the week have supported your decision. Do this for seven weeks. Have you really made that decision?

Summary

- Merely "wanting" something is meaningless. We can spend all day "wanting" to escape from it all, without taking one step toward any outcome. "Wanting" lacks the crucial element of decision.

- Making decisions means daring to set a goal, focusing your energy, and taking full responsibility for all the consequences of what you want.

- The secret of those who are sincerely happy and successful is that they are able to make decisions.

- Unfortunately, many people refuse to make decisions, so they never achieve what they want or get what they wish for. In life, either you decide or life decides for you.

- When you react, you send out passive energy. When you decide to participate in your fate, you send out active energy.

- If you don't decide, you are still creating—only the energy of indecision creates without direction or focus.

Affirmation

I decide that from now on I willnot be attached to my old, limiting thoughts and beliefs. I decide to look at my past patterns calmly and objectively, and I am prepared to make changes. I decide to make today a beautiful day. I decide to live.

In Practice

- Take some time to think about the relationship between the quality of your life and the quality of your choices.

- Ask yourself honestly whether your life is shaped more by others' choices than by your own.

- Be conscious that your happiness, health, and success in your life right now are largely the sum of the decisions that you have made in the past. What aspects of your life can you trace to particular choices? How would your life be different if you had made different decisions?

- Remind yourself that your future happiness, health, and success will largely be determined by the choices and the decisions that you make from now on. Ask yourself whether there is a decision you need to make in your life right now but are afraid to. What consequences of the decision are you afraid of? What are the consequences of not deciding?

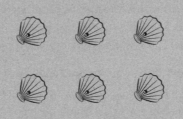

Law 6

RECOGNIZE
YOUR NO-CURRENT

The world around us is a world of effects. So if you only change something in that world, you actually change nothing.

MARIANNE WIILLIAMSON

*I*n 1994 I came into contact with "pathwork," a powerful self-inquiry practice that has helped me understand better how the laws of creation work. Pathwork, also called The Path, is a personal psychological journey that brings you closer to yourself; it is also a way of coming closer to your divine essence, by whatever name you call it. It forms a bridge between psychotherapy and spirituality with its focus on recognizing and changing unconscious patterns as a necessary condition of spiritual life. It is, without a doubt, the most comprehensive and practical tool for self-analysis that I have ever encountered, and it deeply affected my life during the late 1990s.

The Path originated with Eva Pierrakos, who was born in Vienna in 1915. In 1957 she started giving lectures, and a group formed around her that referred to itself as The Path, working with the lectures and the instructions they contained. Pierrakos gave 270 lectures, each on a separate topic, that formed an invaluable body of work. Many of these lectures were transcribed, compiled, and published in book form.

One of the greatest eye-openers for me was in her 125th lecture about the "no-current" and the "yes-current," given on May 29, 1964. In it, Pierrakos explained that even if you want something very strongly and deeply at a conscious level, and even if your conscious attitude toward life is positive, if an unconscious negativity within you—what Pierrakos called a "no-current"—overrides your positive desire, it will be impossible for you to have the life that you want. Without being aware of it, you will be working against yourself and sabotaging your own happiness.

•

Even if your conscious attitude toward life is positive,
an unconscious "no-current" can keep you
from having the life you want.

•

The "yes-current" is life force and creative power. It strives for oneness, harmony, wholeness, and fulfillment and manifests itself as truth and love. The yes-current greets life as it is with joy and gratitude. In her lecture, Pierrakos said, "All those who flow with the 'yes-current' will find themselves in such harmony, will reach higher and higher levels of such perfect beingness, and will extend beyond the experiential bounds of consciousness, undisturbed by ideas that are false and work against one another . . . The 'yes-current' is. It is the root that underlies all that is. It is the Reason, the inner Source, and from that place gives you a realistic understanding of things. You see outer appearances for what they are."

●

The "yes-current" is life force and creative power.
It greets life as it is with joy and gratitude.

●

The no-current is the opposite of the yes-current and therefore works against it. It says no to life, to progress, and to development. The no-current consists of ignorance, unconsciousness, blindness, and lack of self-knowledge. It has its origins in fear and limitation, and it spreads fear and limitation. It is the antithesis of love, of all that leads to inner peace and happiness. The no-current leads to unrest, chaos, and destruction.

If you want to learn to use your creative power effectively, then you must come to terms with your no-current. I meet so many people who say they have an unbelievably positive attitude towards life and yet still they can't find the happiness they long for. Statements like these point to a no-current that has yet to be recognized and acknowledged. At a conscious level, you desperately want something, yet something unconscious keeps it from you. If you don't know what that something is, you can't overcome it. So the very first step is to become aware of the ways in which you approach life negatively, fearfully, or destructively. It's a mistake—and one of the biggest misconceptions of self-development—to think that acknowledging your destructive patterns is a bad thing in itself. Having a positive attitude doesn't mean that you should ignore the negative aspects of yourself. Quite the contrary: to liberate your life force, creative power, and love, you must make contact with your negative side. You can only set your potential for change in motion if you can hear how you say no to the things you long for.

◉

You can only set your potential for change in motion if you can hear how you say no to what you long for.

◉

A striking example of an unacknowledged no-current comes from my close friend Sarah, who recently met the "love of her life." He was independent, intelligent, self-willed, and gorgeous, and she experienced a powerful soul recognition with him. She had butterflies in her stomach, and she knew for sure: *he's the one. This is the man I have always longed for; this is my other half.* She made her feelings clear, and the feelings were mutual. All the ingredients for a successful relationship were there, and everything inside her seemed to scream "Yes!" Despite all this, after two weeks she said to me, "I'm afraid of one thing—I don't know if I can trust my feelings." I remembered this sentence, because I heard a no-current. Sarah was vaguely aware of it, but she had yet to recognize its latent destructive power.

●

The no-current is the opposite of the yes-current and therefore works against it. It says no to life, to development, and to progress.

●

Madly in love, Sarah went away with her new flame for a week. After that, I didn't hear from her for weeks. When I called her one day to ask how things had gone, she sounded downhearted. It turned out that she had already ended the relationship, after only a few weeks. "I don't know if my feelings for him are strong enough," she said. "I thought it was strange that when I came home I didn't have the feeling that I wanted to be with him whatever happened. And I'm not sure if he's going to bring me the peace I'm looking for. Oh, maybe I'm just the eternal single—I've noticed that I'm very attached to my freedom and independence after all."

"But now you're saying exactly the same things as you did about all the men you went out with before this one," I told her. "How many men have to come along before you're brave enough to face your own defense mechanisms and see how you keep saying no to the very thing you want so much?"

This is often how it goes. You wish for something, and it comes into your path. The question then is whether you are you capable of recognizing it and seizing it. This depends entirely on whether your yes-current is flowing freely and not being countered by a no-current. That's why it is so important for you to uncover and accept your hidden attitudes if you are to understand why something always seems to be lacking in your life. Of course Sarah didn't trust her own feelings; how can you trust your feelings if you don't even know yourself completely?

●

You wish for something,
and it comes into your path. The question then is
whether you are capable of seizing it.

●

The difficult thing about dealing with the no-current is that for someone who hasn't yet acknowledged his or her unconscious negativity, the no-current can actually feel like a step in the right direction—positive and liberating.

My friend experienced immediate peace and freedom when she came home and drew her onclusion. "See," she said, "I feel better now, so he can't be the one."

And when the longing to meet that one true partner arises again and leads her into another relationship, the pattern will start again, and she will again run up against her unconscious resistance. And when she does, she will fool herself again and decide after a few weeks that he's not the one after all. She will not understand why she can't get the love she longs for, because she is looking for the reasons in the wrong place: outside herself.

•

For someone who hasn't yet acknowledged his or her unconscious negativity, the no-current can feel positive and liberating, like a step in the right direction.

•

Many people shy away from what they want most of all in order to avoid the pain of failing, or, perhaps worse, of achieving their desire and then losing it again. It is the responsibility for their own wishes that they are walking away from. Later they may say, "See, I failed again. I'm better off on my own" or "I'm not meant to be happy" or "I wasn't born to succeed." They don't see that everything inside them, on an unconscious level, is working to confirm that preconceived idea.

•

It is the responsibility for your own wish that you are walking away from. Later you'll be able to say, "See, I failed again."

•

This is the reason behind much of our misery and confusion: we are ignorant of our own power to create and unaware that we are creating our experience all the time, whether we know it or not. Whether or not you realize that you want something is beside the point: you create with both your conscious will and your unconscious will. And when you want two different things—when your conscious will and unconscious will oppose each other— the opposition causes inner conflict and pain. Your unconscious will is generating real, tangible life experiences that you can't explain logically with your conscious mind; you just think that your life situation is not giving you what you want.

You have to learn to be aware of your unconscious

motives, because your unconscious continues creating to its heart's content underneath the surface, even while on a conscious level you may want other things. But how can you become conscious of thoughts that are unconscious? In the same way that you perceive your conscious thoughts: by focusing on how you use them. Once you start allowing your confused and conflicting feelings to arise and paying attention to the thought patterns around them, you will see any situation for what it truly is: your own creation. When you see this, you are no longer helpless. You are in a position to transform, because you are looking for the cause of your lack in the right place: inside yourself.

Sometimes, even if you recognize and are determined to overcome your negative, destructive attitudes, with all the will in the world still you do not seem to be able to change them. Deeply buried ideas are at work here, unconscious conclusions that you may have drawn a very long time ago.

Bring your no-current to light

Most of us are not conscious of our own destructiveness. If you have what you consider a positive attitude, you probably think that rules out any inner negativity, and if you have no inner negativity, you don't need to give it any attention. But wherever lack, confusion, or dissatisfaction is present, there is a no-current at work that you must bring to light in order to counter it.

One tool for mapping out your unconscious negativity is to keep a written record of your thoughts and reactions to people and events. If you write down your difficulties with life and relationships honestly, without censoring yourself, at some point you will discover a pattern—a common denominator such as an emotional trigger, a self-criticism, or even a particular phrase that shows up again and again in your notes. You probably won't see this right away. You may not think it's there at all. But if you continue systematically searching for the patterns in your problems you will eventually find that common denominator—even if it takes a few months. It's a key to your unconscious processes, which in turn points you to the long-held ideas and incorrect "conclusions" that you may have formed early in life. This is where the root of your problems can be found, and also the starting point for dealing with them constructively.

◉

When you tune in to the way you say no to the things you really long for, you are no longer able to live in doubt, fear, and misery.

◉

We all form certain impressions throughout our life, starting in childhood. These impressions arise as a result of the people and influences in our environment, as well as events that led us to conclusions about the world and about ourselves. Obviously, when you're young, you don't form these impressions in a well-thought-out or reasoned way. Instead you take your impressions by way of emotional reactions, which can color your whole approach to life. As a child, you don't yet have the frame of reference to know if an event or experience is good or bad, normal or abnormal. So when you have an unpleasant experience, you start thinking that this is the norm, and certain ideas begin to creep in: for example, that enjoyment is followed by punishment, or that other people's problems are your fault. Over time, these ideas, attitudes, and conclusions embed themselves deeply within your unconscious, where they work unseen to shape your life as it is now.

As you get older, the unconscious emotional knowledge that these ideas—often referred to as "images"—form conflicts with the intellectual knowledge that you have built up over the years. So although your thoughts may all be positive and constructive, your hidden consciousness can contradict what your conscious mind is doing and keep you from being happy, successful, and healthy. You may even think you're leading a highly conscious life, without seeing that you keep treating yourself the same way you did when you were a child, or the way your unconscious considers "normal," ideas according to your old, destructive patterns. It is precisely because those old patterns and ideas are at once so ingrained and so invisible to you that letting go of them is so difficult. But the moment you start to understand where these patterns originate, their repetition starts to lose momentum. As soon as you recognize where your actions and reactions come from, negativity loses its power.

Once you've recognized the no-current, you'll never be the same again. You will have taken a huge step forward in your personal development, your relationships, and your vision of life. When you tune in to the way you say no to the things you really long for, you are no longer able to live in doubt, fear, and misery. At that point you cease to be helpless in your own life and come into real contact with the truth and order of the universe.

●

Once you've recognized the no-current, you'll never be the same again. You will come into real contact with the truth and order of the universe.

●

Summary

- The "yes-current" is life force and creative power. It manifests itself as truth and love.

- The "no-current" is the opposite of the yes-current and therefore works against it. It says no to life, to progress, and to development. It consists of of unconsciousness, ignorance, blindness, and lack of self-knowledge.

- If you want to learn to use your creative power effectively, it is essential that you bring your no-current to light. You can only set your potential for change in motion if you can hear how you say no to what you so desperately wish and long for.

- Whether or not you realize that you want something is beside the point; you create with both your conscious will and your unconscious will.

- When you uncover the unconscious ideas and images that give rise to your actions and reactions, then negativity loses its power.

Affirmation

Everything in my life is a reflection of who I am in this moment. I recognize my own influence on my difficulties, disappointments, and lack. I no longer look outside myself for causes and solutions, but turn the searchlight within. When I do this, I banish my helplessness and step into my power.

In practice

- Ask yourself these questions: Am I the person I want to be in this moment? Am I leading the life I want to live now? If you answer "No" to either question, then you must acknowledge that you have an inner "no-current," an unconscious negativity that makes you self-destructive.

- Ask yourself if you have been blaming causes outside yourself for the fact that you lack things you want. Look at your own actions, emotions, and attitudes honestly and objectively so you can uncover your inner blocks.

- Resolve to approach the difficult and painful experiences in your life as opportunities for taking a look at yourself and questioning what your part in these situations is. What patterns of action or reaction do you find yourself repeating?

- Look at the part of you that is afraid of being hurt or failing. Try to uncover the beliefs and images from your childhood that give rise to this fear.

- Write down your thoughts and feelings about challenging situations and relationships. Look for a common denominator that will point you to your unconscious processes. Even if it takes time, be patient; the pattern will emerge.

Law 7

 # LEARN
TO LET GO

Letting go is having the courage to allow
the truth to come about.

THE DEEPER SECRET

*R*ecently, I read an interesting interview with a woman named Marilyn Sherman in the journal of the National Speakers Association. The headline of the article got my attention: "Whose comfort zone are you in?"

She explained that some years ago she had had a secure and well-paid job as a corporate trainer, but that her dream was to become self-employed as a professional speaker. When she discussed it with her father, whom she considered her mentor, he asked her what she could count on if she went out on her own. Did she have any commitments from companies that wanted to engage her as a speaker? When she said no, he advised her against taking the plunge. Despite this, she plucked up all her courage and decided to turn her greatest dream into reality. Not long after, the company that she had thought would give her long-term security was sold and all its employees were forced to look for other jobs.

In the interview, Sherman recalled how she often told this story to her audiences when she spoke, following it up with a rhetorical question: "Can you imagine what would have happened if I'd stayed in my comfort zone, just because my father had said what a good job I had?" One day, a woman in the audience answered her: "If you'd stayed with that company, you'd have been living in your father's comfort zone, not yours."

●

Deciding to seek what you want in your life means being prepared to leave your comfort zone.

●

Deciding to seek what you want in your life means being prepared to leave your comfort zone. The boundaries of this comfort zone are delineated by what you know—those familiar ideas and assumptions you have received and unconsciously absorbed from your parents or educators. It is a pattern that you try to duplicate time and time again in your adult life because it seems "safe." But as a rule, the comfort zone is not that safe, or even all that comfortable. In fact, in your comfort zone you are a prisoner of your own limiting beliefs and fears—perhaps a fear of change, a lack of self-worth, or a buried conviction that you don't have the right to exist. These make the comfort zone an extremely oppressive place.

◉

Deciding is breaking through safe, predictable boundaries.

◉

In earlier chapters, we talked about how limiting beliefs and unconscious patterns of negativity can stand between you and your dreams. To step outside your comfort zone means taking active steps to let go of those patterns and beliefs and give up the false safety of the familiar. So, in essence, deciding is inextricably bound to letting go. That's why so many people are so indecisive, because letting go is something that most people prefer not to do. Letting go is scary, because it is often accompanied by pain—the pain of separating from old ideas, assurances, hopes, and dreams—and most people prefer to hang on to their old, familiar patterns, however negative or destructive those may be. The known is familiar and the outcome of old patterns is predictable. This keeps you from being confronted with surprises, so you think you've figured out how to avoid pain. The problem arises when you are not prepared to let go of your comfort zone, but you want to change your life at the same time. The two are not compatible, so you will have to make a choice. It will have to be one or the other.

You cannot choose anything without letting go of something else. For instance, my friend Robert is faced with making certain decisions that will affect his inner growth and the development of his potential. He is holding back from making these decisions because he says he is afraid of coming into conflict with people around him and their expectations of him. Obviously, what he really fears is losing face or failing. If Robert really decides to stand up for himself, his own aspirations, his wishes and dreams, he will have to let go of his intention not to be at odds with others and be honest about his deeper fear. Being honest is an act of regeneration that sets a huge amount of positive energy in motion. You cannot bring change into your life if you have not grounded yourself in your current reality, because you cannot create anything outside of reality.

Sometimes the things you must let go of are more concrete. Another friend recently said to me, "When I had my son, I knew right from the beginning that I was not prepared to give up anything for motherhood. I wanted to keep my international job, continue to play sports, and enjoy everything that life had to offer." Now she has come to a point in her life where life is choosing for her: her job is uncertain, her relationship is coming to an end, her son has problems at school, and she is desperately struggling with her health.

●

You cannot choose anything without letting go of something else.

●

And this is true for many of us: we want a family, a fulfilling relationship, a successful career, and a social life, and we'd like to look healthy and youthful while we're at it. And we want all of this without crossing any option off the list. It is theoretically possible that someone might succeed in this, although I don't know anyone who has. It's certainly not true that if you want something badly enough, and you think positively enough, visualize powerfully enough, that the universe will give you everything you want. The law of creation doesn't work like that. Sometimes you just need to realize that if you want to achieve one thing, you have to let go of something else.

But the good news is that, ultimately, the pain—which comes from letting go—is always accompanied by a sense of liberation and new space. By letting go of limiting beliefs, you create the space to realize your dreams. In addition, letting go enables you to create focus: you let other things go so that you can focus totally on what it is that you want. Deciding means defining what you want most and accepting the consequences.

•

"I want to, but I can't."
How often do we say that?

•

It all comes down to this: in order to get what you want in life, you will have to let go of all the attachments that have held you back from it until now. Everyone has a dream. If you have not yet made that dream a reality, it's because of the limiting thoughts and beliefs that you have placed between yourself and your dream. One woman I know is a good example of this. She works as a coach at a major insurance company and dreams of being a spiritual leader in her workplace. The spectrum of limiting thoughts that she places between herself and the realization of her dream is endless: "I want to, but it's just not possible in this company. It's impossible with this team of people. It won't work with this manager. This or that policy won't allow it." *I want to, but I can't.* How often do we say that? Wishing in this way means you are afraid of reality and afraid to let go. The woman in this example is staying in her comfort zone. She is holding on to her limiting beliefs so that she won't have to face the consequences of what she wants and the decision she has made. This means that she doesn't need to risk failure, feel uncertain, or have any fear of what the future may bring. Since it's not going to happen anyway, she doesn't have to stand up for it. Maybe another time, in another place, with other people—but not now.

Making the decision to pursue what you want means letting go in many ways—of your familiar comfort zone, of your resistance to life's natural flow, of the other things you would like to have at the same time. Wanting by itself isn't scary. Deciding is scarier. Making your dreams a reality is the scariest thing of all. Ultimately, what you are letting go of is fear, or, more precisely, the power that fear has to control you. As one classic self-help guide put it, in a credo that's lived by leaders such as Jimmy Choo founder Tamara Mellon: "Feel the fear and do it anyway." Fear is there not to be denied, but to be faced. You can feel fear and still not let it lead you. The true path to letting go is acceptance.

●

In order to get what you want in life, you will have to let go of all the atachments that have held you back from it until now.

●

Summary

- Deciding means being prepared to leave your comfort zone.

- Most people prefer to hang on to their old, familiar patterns, however negative or destructive they may be, because the outcome of old patterns is predictable and therefore "safe."

- You know that limiting beliefs can hold you back. To step outside your comfort zone means taking active steps to let go of those beliefs.

- You cannot choose anything without letting go of something else. Letting go gives you space to focus totally on what you want most.

- In order to get what you want in life, you will have to let go of all the ideas that have held you back until now.

Affirmation

I recognize my negative patterns, and I decide to change them. I let go of my resistance and my fear. Limiting thoughts no longer hold any power over me.
I am the power in my world.

In practice

- Take a close look at your comfort zone. Are you truly comfortable within it? Or are those familiar boundaries keeping you from living freely?

- Remind yourself every day that it is possible to change limiting thought patterns and, by doing so, create different experiences in your life.

- Practice recognizing and examining the thought patterns that may be standing between you and what you want. Can you imagine ways to transform them into more positive and constructive ones?

- If you feel afraid, don't judge yourself for it, but remember that you don't have to act accordingly. It's all right to be afraid of letting go, but you don't need to let your fear lead you.

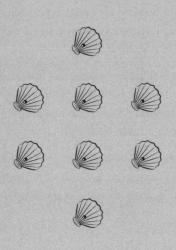

Law 8

LIVE
IN THE NOW

Imagine the earth without any human life, only
inhabited by plants and animals. Would there
be a past and a future then? Would we be able to
talk about time in a meaningful way? If someone
was able to ask the questions what time is it, or
what day is it, they would be meaningless. These
questions would be bewildering for the oak and
the eagle. "Well, it's Now, of course. It's Now.
What else is there?"

ECKHART TOLLE

*T*he real secret of many people who are able to create the life they were born to live is that they know the value of the present moment. They allow themselves to live life *now*—even if life at this moment is anything but perfect. If you always want to be somewhere other than where you are now, you are denying your value and power in the present moment, and therefore your life. You cannot make change or reach fulfillment in life from a place of denial. You cannot create anything outside of the here and now.

•

People who create the life they were born to live know the value of the present moment, even if life at this moment is far from perfect.

•

In a television program I watched about *The Secret*, some people who were attending workshops shared their thoughts and experiences. I noticed one thing in particular: most of them were discontented and felt that their present lives were lacking. They hoped that *The Secret* would help them find a way out, that it would release them from the imperfect here and now. They all wanted something other than what their present lives had to offer. This is no surprise, since *The Secret* seems to promise that you can have anything you want in life. But the first step, the real secret, is to learn to want what you have. You cannot use your creative power to sidestep reality and dismiss or deny the here and now; that's not how creation works. As Eckhart Tolle writes in *The Power of Now*: "Have you ever experienced, done, thought, or felt anything outside of the Now? Do you think that you could ever do this? Can anything actually happen outside of the Now? Nothing ever happened in the past; it happened in the Now. Nothing will ever happen in the future; all future events take place in the Now."

•

The Secret seems to promise that you can have anything you want in life. But the first step, the real secret, is to learn to want what you have.

•

●

You cannot use your creative power to side-step reality
and dismiss or deny the here and now.
That's not how creation works.

●

Embracing reality with gratitude is an act of regeneration. However much it may seem otherwise, it is in the reality of the here and now that the real beauty of life and love can be found. It is no accident that for Buddhists, being completely present in the moment is the definition of experiencing God. From that place of contact with God—or your divine essence or greater self—you connect with your real creative power. And to ground yourself in the reality of the here and now, you need to surrender. Surrender means letting go of your illusory control over events and detaching yourself from your preconceived notions of how your life ought to be. It means saying farewell to all the dreams and illusions of the mind. Behind those dreams and illusions lies your space for change and new creation.

In my own life, things rarely went as I had hoped, expected, or imagined. As a result, I learned that being open to the reality of life, without judging life, leads to a deeper level of trust: the trust that everything that happens in your life is right for you and your path. Each time you successfully experience an event in this way, it feels like a huge inner step forward, and your faith in your own power grows.

●

Surrendering means saying farewell to all the dreams and illusions of the mind. Behind them lies your space for change and new creation.

●

Many of us are born saboteurs of the here and now. Experiencing love and happiness is simply too frightening at close range. Just look around: how many people do you know who have been saying for years how happy they are, yet still say how happy they would like to be? Watch closely how, when the opportunity for happiness presents itself in the here and now, they blow these chances, walk away from them, or let them pass by.

●

The opportunities, possibilities, and happiness of the present moment are so close at hand that we barely experience them as real.

●

This is why many people think that *The Secret* does not work for them. They don't see the connection between their tangible experiences and their unconscious inner beliefs and processes. If they hold the unconscious inner belief "I don't deserve it," they will always align their outer circumstances with this inner reality. As an example, let's say you have a wish list for your ideal partner, and a partner with all those qualities shows up on your doorstep tomorrow. If you are still guided by your inner belief that happiness is not meant for you, that this is why you haven't found the love you want, and that none of your desires will be fulfilled anyway, then you will quickly find plenty of so-called reasons why this partner is not "the one." Because you unconsciously think that you are unworthy or undeserving, you will always deeply mistrust, push away, or even destroy the happiness that presents itself in the here and now. Or you will deceive yourself by thinking, "I'm not ready for this yet." This is why many people desire happiness, but don't really have the desire to realize that dream. We would rather lose ourselves in hope, dreams, and expectations than face our fears like true heroes and experience the love and happiness already present in the here and now.

◉

Building your trust starts with letting go of your false beliefs, false hope, and false faith, which lie like a suffocating blanket over the beauty of the Now.

◉

The opportunities, possibilities, and happiness of now are so close at hand that we barely experience them as real. We think that something so accessible cannot possibly be of any value. "The soul is an enormous space and a lot of it is darkness," so said Iris Murdoch in Anne Bancroft's *Women in Search of the Sacred*. "Living in the Now means a deep confrontation with that darkness. Living in the Now is therefore uncompromising—equally as uncompromising as love." It takes trust to take that plunge into the darkness.

This is perhaps one of the most difficult elements of the law of creation, but also one of the most important. And because that trust is so hard to come by, our battle with the Now is an eternal theme in literature and films as well as in our lives. We are always taking to our heels in the belief that we can escape from reality to something better, more beautiful, and more right for us. Our flight leaves a trail of destruction through the landscape of happiness and gouges gaping holes in our self-esteem. Psychology refers to this pattern as a "fear of intimacy" or "fear of commitment," but the underlying problem is a lack of trust.

Building your trust starts with letting go of your false beliefs, false hope, and false faith, which lie like a suffocating blanket over the beauty of the Now. They leave no room for trusting in the value and worth of reality, or for the knowledge that things are as they are for a very good reason. Trusting is knowing with your heart. You listen to your heart by seeking out the silence. The silence is the current that carries you to the deepest core of your being, where you come to know who you are and experience the fullness of your inner power.

Summary

- Learning to use your creative power has everything to do with living in the here and now.

- *The Secret* promises that you can have anything you want in life, but the first step is to learn to want what you have.

- Using your creative power to sidestep the truth and dismiss or deny the here and now is an impossible task.

- You cannot do, think, or feel anything outside of the Now. Nothing can happen outside of the Now. Nothing ever happened in the past; nothing will ever happen in the future; all events, past and future, take place in the Now.

- To ground yourself in the reality of here and now, you need to surrender your so-called control over events and detach yourself from your prejudices and preconceived ideas about how your life ought to be.

- To live in the here and now calls for profound trust. You build trust by letting go of your false beliefs, false hope, and false faith, which mask the reality and beauty of the Now and keep you from seeing that everything is as it is for a reason.

Affirmation

I live in the Now. I love life as it is Now. I do not banish my love and attention to the past or to the future. My future does not yet exist; what I do Now creates my future. My attention is focused on what I can do today.

In practice

- Every day for a week, write down how often your mind wanders from where you are and what is happening in a given moment. How often do you find yourself dwelling on something that has already happened or thinking ahead to what's yet to come?

- Ask yourself whether you are more comfortable being "on your way" to something than really experiencing what is going on right now. Are you putting off taking some action in your life until an unspecified future time when the conditions will be right?

- Think about ways you may be sabotaging the here and now. How often do you make excuses for not living and loving in the moment?

- Resolve to spend a week in the here and now, to see the world and love it as it is now.

- As an experiment, decide not to complain about anything for a week, but to fully accept what is.

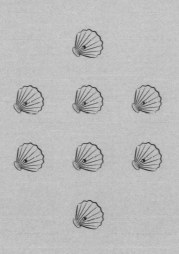

Taking Responsibility

Law 9

ACCEPT YOUR
ACCOUNTABILITY

Ordinary life can be a prison, unless you take
responsibility for yourself.

ELAINE McINNES

Wanting takes place in three stages. It means first coming to a full understanding of what you want and why, then deciding to actively seek it, and, finally, being prepared to take full responsibility for all the consequences of your decision. Taking responsibility means that each time you run up against limitations, or encounter resistance from within or without, you are prepared to focus the searchlight inwards in order to clear the blocks that keep you from creating the life you were born to live.

•

Many people watch reality from the sidelines, hoping that something from outside will one day save them.

•

It may seem as though you could save yourself this trouble by believing in a magical solution—something that would give you everything you wanted from the outside, if you just wanted it badly enough. But in reality, if you take this attitude to life, you are turning yourself over to outside influences and relinquishing your power over your own future. Not accepting that you are responsible for your own happiness and well-being is an immature view of life, based on a child's simplistic image of the world. The child in you expects its wishes and needs to be met unconditionally, holds others responsible for its well-being and happiness, and unconsciously uses outside events and the behavior of others as an excuse for not doing the work it takes to be happy. "People aren't nice to me. See, I can't be happy!"

Many people don't participate fully in their lives in a mature and responsible way. Instead, they watch reality from the sidelines, hoping that something from outside will one day rescue them, be it the ideal partner, the perfect job, or salvation in some other form. Anytime they are hurt, they retreat to their comfort zone and blame the outside world, which leads them to withdraw even more from real life. "See!" they say. "The law of attraction works for everyone except me." The reason the laws of the universe don't work for these people is that they have distanced themselves from their own creative power. Because they do not trust themselves, they have no trust in their power, so they unconsciously give their power away to things outside themselves. They don't yet understand that this behavior is not rewarded. It's only when you step fully into life, facing your fears and accepting reality, that the primordial powers of the universe can be unleashed to work on your behalf. To embrace life in this way, you need to be prepared to make mistakes and to learn by them; this means that you must want—and dare—to experience what is.

It is only when you step fully into life, facing your fears, that the primordial powers of the universe can be unleashed to work on your behalf.

Taking responsibility for yourself is acknowledging the connection between your inner beliefs and your outer circumstances. It is recognizing that to a large extent you create your reality with your thoughts, attitudes, and patterns of feeling—not only for ill, but for good. And, further, taking responsibility for yourself is liberating yourself from the sway of your unconscious negativity. It is knowing that you can choose different patterns of feeling and thinking at any moment, that you can choose to struggle against the flow of life or to surrender to it, deciding from now on that you will stand at the helm of your life.

When you do this, you free yourself from unhealthy forms of dependency and victimhood in many areas of your life, such as your personal relationships. A lack of self-responsibility can turn us into unattractive and unappealing people, and it can throw relationships seriously off course. If you do not take responsibility for yourself within a relationship, then you find yourself resorting to demands, expectations, and criticism in an effort to make the other person give you what you need. All too often, you end up exploiting the other person emotionally, because the relationship comes to be based on needing instead of loving and on claiming instead of choosing freely to be together.

Putting a stop to complaints and accusations, no longer playing the role of victim or reproaching yourself, and taking action even if you don't want to—these form the basis of self-responsibility. If you are not living a life that makes you happy now, then you can do one of three things: make the decision to change your life; fully accept your life as it is; or withdraw from life as a victim and sit in the corner moping. No matter what the situation, if you want to take responsibility for your life you will have to choose one of these three options.

If you call on the universe for help, it can only assist you on one condition: that you really have committed to be captain of your ship. By taking responsibility for yourself, you connect yourself with your creative power and, in turn, with the power of the universe. You determine the direction in which that power will work on your behalf. The universe cannot help you until you have done this.

●

Putting a stop to complaints and accusations, no longer playing the role of victim or reproaching yourself, and taking action even if you do not want to——these form the basis of self-responsibility.

●

Summary

- Accepting your own accountability is recognizing the connection between your inner beliefs and your outer circumstances. It is recognizing that you create your reality with your thoughts, attitudes, and patterns of feeling —both for ill and for good.

- Accepting your own accountability means that each time you encounter limitations or resistance, you are prepared to direct the searchlight inwards to find its source and overcome it.

- When you take responsibility for yourself, you know that you can choose other patterns of feeling and thinking at any moment, and that you can choose to struggle against the current of life or to surrender to it. You decide that from now on you will stand at the helm of your life.

- Putting a stop to complaints and accusations, no longer playing the role of victim or reproaching yourself, and taking action even if you do not want to—these form the basis of self-responsibility.

- If you are not living a life that makes you happy now, then you can do one of three things: make the decision to change your life; fully accept your life as it is; or withdraw from life as a victim and sit in the corner moping.

- You call on the help of the universe, it can only help you on the condition that you really have made the commitment to be captain of your ship.

- By taking responsibility for yourself, you connect yourself with your creative power and, in turn, with the power of the universe. You determine the direction in which that power will work on your behalf. The universe cannot help you until you have done this.

Affirmation

*I am responsible for my happiness and well-being.
I recognize the direct connection between my inner beliefs
and my lacks and difficulties. I recognize that
I contribute to creating all circumstances, situations,
and events in my life with my thoughts,
attitudes, and feelings.*

In Practice

- Ask yourself honestly whether you are inclined to place the responsibility for your personal happiness and well-being in the hands of others. For example, do you imagine you would be happy if only your partner would change?

- Ask yourself whether, and how, you blame outside factors and circumstances for your lack of success, inner peace, or happiness.

- Look for at least one situation in your life in which you see a direct connection between your inner beliefs, thoughts, and attitudes and your dissatisfaction, lack, or difficulties.

- Practice reminding yourself that what happens outside you is a direct reflection of what is happing on the inside, and that every relationship is a mirror of your relationship with yourself.

- Refrain from complaining, reproaching yourself, and pointing to others as the reasons for your dissatisfaction or unhappiness for seven weeks. On the same day each week, write down honestly what certain situations and relationships in your life right now tell you about yourself, your beliefs, and your patterns of feeling and thinking.

Law 10

SOLIDIFY YOUR
SELF-ESTEEM

He who lives in harmony with himself,
lives in harmony with the universe.

MARCUS AURELIUS

*T*rusting in the way the laws of creation work has everything to do with trusting in yourself and your own creative power. Whatever you wish for, if you believe deep inside that you are not worth it and do not deserve it, then you are not open to receiving it and you cannot possibly trust in your power to create it.

●

Without healthy self-esteem, you may understand how the laws of creation work, but you will not be able to work with them.

●

I have been fascinated by the themes of self-esteem and self-respect for years and have written about them for almost as long. To me, it's clear that they are at the heart of a person's development. The life that you are seeking is intimately connected to what you think about yourself and wish for yourself on a deep inner level. Whether you are searching for inner peace, looking for love, or trying to be healthier, your search must begin with the inner belief that you are worth it—that you deserve abundance in life! If you do not value or respect yourself enough, an unconscious voice inside you will always say, "I don't deserve happiness." When good things come into your path, you will be unable to embrace them.

The mechanism of self-esteem is crucial to the functioning of the laws of creation; truly, it makes or breaks the game. Without healthy self-esteem, you may grasp those laws and understand perfectly well how they operate, but you will not be able to work with them. To get what you wish for, you must want things from a place of self-esteem and self-respect. The universe is quite clear on this point. If you're hoping that achieving what you seek will *give* you self-esteem and self-respect, that won't work—the universe knows the difference, and you'll end up back at square one every time.

●

*Because we create our outer world from our inner world,
our self-image is often our fate.*

●

Because we create a large part of our outer world from
our inner world, our self-image is often our fate. Time and
time again, you will create the life that mirrors your idea
of your own self-worth. If you have too little self-esteem,
your thoughts, unconscious or conscious, will be negative
and destructive, which will cause you to attract negative
life experiences and events. On the other hand, if you
have a strong sense of self-esteem, your thoughts will be
positive and constructive, which will cause you to create
positive experiences and circumstances. A healthy sense
of self-esteem enables you to trust yourself when making
decisions, to act in line with your intuition, to express
yourself, and to take responsibility for your happiness and
well-being. Self-esteem connects you with your inner fire

so you can make deliberate use of the creative power within you. It leaves an indelible mark on your daily life, your relationships, your success, and your happiness; without self-esteem, you lack the power and the trust to take your place in the world.

●

Change always begins on the inside, and outer circumstances transform themselves accordingly.

●

Most people are not aware of the force of their inner beliefs, let alone the way in which they are constantly turning these beliefs into tangible experience. To receive what you long for in life, you must come to terms with your inner reality. In the first place, you need the courage to look at yourself and your life without judgment, without blaming other people or circumstances, and without guilt or self-reproach. Only by opening your eyes to the full reality of your world, the truth of who you are now and where you are now, will you become more conscious of your inner beliefs and judgments about yourself, the thoughts that you allow, the feelings that you have, and the reactions to people and events that arise from all these. If you could take half of the time and energy that you spend trying to change your circumstances and use it to work on discerning your inner patterns then your relationship with yourself would deepen in understanding and the universe would respond with sympathy. Nothing in your life can change without something first changing inside you.

◉

Time and time again, you create the life that mirrors your idea of your own self-worth.

◉

I recently received a letter from a teacher, who wrote, "I have all your books, and I read certain passages over and over. I know that it is important for me to learn to love myself more as I am. But I am still insecure and always think that other people are more powerful, beautiful, and intelligent. This is a really big problem in my relationship, because it's driving my boyfriend crazy. How can I start loving myself more? How do I actually do it?"

I wrote back to her and explained that there are seven important conditions for self-esteem, including the factors that lower or raise your sense of self-worth, the outside influences on you, the influence of your inner world, and the places where these two meet. I also describe these conditions in *Making Love*. You can use these points to measure the state of your self-esteem right now and also to work on enhancing it.

THEY ARE:

1. *Take responsibility for yourself.* Don't look to people or things outside yourself to make you feel good about what and who you are.

2. *Accept yourself.* Do you think you can't be happy until something about you changes? Imagine embracing that part of you, not resignedly, but gladly.

3. *Live in the here and now.* If you're always looking ahead to tomorrow or gazing back at yesterday, it stands to reason you won't feel good about your life today.

4. *Stand up for yourself.* Are there people in your life who treat you disrespectfully or create difficulties for you? Tolerating such treatment can erode your sense of yourself.

5. *Be true to yourself.* The more you act in alignment with your most important values and in tune with your deepest self, the better you will feel about the way you're living.

6. *Live purposefully.* You know how discouraging it is to wander aimlessly, wasting time, when you're trying to get somewhere important. It's the same with your path of life.

7. *Have faith.* If you believe in yourself, all things are possible.

The degree to which you make these points a part of your life is the degree to which you will strengthen and support your sense of self-esteem. And conversely, if you ignore these points then you will weaken or sabotage it to the same degree. These seven points can often bring about unique and major changes.

•

Nothing in your life can change without something first changing inside you.

•

Ultimately, the choice is yours. You can choose to fight against yourself by playing the victim or indulging in self-pity and bitterness, or you can choose to love and value yourself. If you choose the latter, then you are choosing to accept yourself completely, just as you are now. Maybe you can't see any reason at all to value yourself at this moment—you think you're too fat, too undisciplined, too lazy, weak, ugly, or manipulative. Maybe at this moment you think you're the biggest loser in the world. But to develop self-esteem, you're going to have to learn to accept the parts of yourself that you judge so harshly.

This is where the great secret of self-esteem really lies: you may think that you can't love or value yourself until you change the things you dislike about yourself, but it's actually the other way around. The fact of the matter is that you cannot develop without acceptance; you cannot change anything that you haven't recognized as being in you or coming from you. If you refuse to accept that you sometimes act irresponsibly, then how will you ever learn to live more responsibly? If you deny that you're afraid of certain things, then how can you overcome your fear? How can you correct the mistakes you make or stop doing harm to other people if you don't admit that you're doing anything wrong? You cannot change a quality whose very existence you deny. You can only change when you give yourself full permission to be who you are and where you are in this moment. *Now*.

When you choose to love and value yourself exactly as

you are now, you step into your own power and connect yourself with the power of the universe. To fully accept who you are now unleashes an incredibly positive force. The energy that you'd otherwise put into fighting with yourself, by way of of self-criticism, perfectionism, and guilt, is now available for you to use in developing your self-esteem. This is positive creative energy, which strengthens the "magnet" in you that attracts the experiences and encounters you need in order to live the life you long for. It's like the saying: you can't love somebody else if you don't love yourself. Likewise, you must love yourself to be able to attract love, and you must love yourself to be able to receive love.

●

You may think you can't love yourself until you change the parts of yourself you judge most harshly. In fact, it's the other way around.

●

If you look at people with fulfilling lives and inspiring relationships, you will notice that they radiate a certain charisma. Their charisma is the result of a well-developed sense of self-esteem. These people stand in their own power. They are clear about their personal boundaries, because they know themselves and stay true to themselves. The energy they radiate naturally attracts worthy people without any particular effort on their part. As your sense of self-esteem increases, and you begin to stand up for yourself, you will notice that you too create your own magnetism. People who previously seemed indifferent or out of reach will react to you in a whole new way.

●

You attract what you are.

●

When you are true to yourself, you attract everything that is in harmony with that self. When you no longer lie to yourself or give your power away, you will have the courage to express what you really want and long for, and you will dare to trust in your own judgment, intuition, and creative power. You will never consciously make a decision that go against your best interests or unconsciously attract situations that are wrong for you. You will set appropriate boundaries in your relationships with others at the right time and withdraw from relationships and situations that do not honor you.

When you have developed a healthy self-esteem, you will draw the perfect abundance of life to you without any effort at all. At the moment you accept yourself as you are and life as it is, you will enter into an equal partnership with the universe, because you will be prepared to participate fully in your fate.

◦

When you choose to love and value yourself exactly as you are now, you step into your own power and connect yourself with the power of the universe.

◦

Summary

- Whether you are searching for inner peace, looking for love, or trying to be healthier, your search must begin with the inner belief that you are worth it and that you deserve abundance in life!

- The mechanism of self-esteem and self-respect is essential to the functioning of the laws of creation. Without a healthy feeling of self-esteem, you may grasp the laws of creation and understand how they work, but you will not be able to work with them.

- Because we largely create our outer world from our inner world, our self-image is often our fate. Time and time again, you will create the life that exactly mirrors your idea of your own self-worth.

- If you have too little self-esteem, your thoughts, conscious or unconscious, will be negative and destructive, which will cause you to attract negative experiences and events. If you have a strong sense of self-esteem, your thoughts will be positive and constructive, which will cause you to create positive circumstances.

- Self-esteem gives you the power to trust yourself in making decisions, to act in line with your intuition, to express yourself, and to take your place in life. It connects you with your inner fire and allows you to make deliberate use of the creative power that you are.

- To develop self-esteem, you must learn to accept the parts of yourself that you judge most harshly. When you do, you turn the energy of self-criticism and blame into positive creative energy that attracts the experiences you want and need to live the life you long for.

Affirmation

I treat myself with understanding and respect in every situation and in every encounter with others. I choose to love and value myself. I choose to allow myself to be treated with respect and appreciation. I embrace my life as it is now. I love myself exactly as I am now.

In Practice

- Take a close, compassionate look at the parts of yourself or your life as it is now that you don't like. Allow yourself to bring to mind the feelings, thoughts, or memories that you think you can hardly bear: these might include fear, uncertainty, shame, sadness, jealousy, humiliation, worry, or anger. Write them down.

- Resolve that for seven weeks you will deny or dismiss these aspects of yourself or your life, but accept them as part of your reality, experience them fully, and look at them without judgement. Say to yourself, "What is, is: everything has the right to be in my world."

- Resolve that for seven weeks you will allow yourself to experience your most difficult feelings without judging or suppressing them. When you begin to feel, for example, anger or jealousy, try to bring the feeling into focus by paying attention to it until it rises to the surface. Don't try to keep yourself from feeling it; say to yourself, "If the feeling exists, then it exists." If you feel resistance to the feeling, accept your resistance; that's a feeling too.

- Every day for seven weeks, look in the mirror. As you do, remind yourself that even if you don't find everything about your outward appearance beautiful, and even if you don't like everything you see when you look inside, you can still have the courage to say, "This is who I am now, and I accept and value myself as I am now. I respect reality as it is now."

Law 11

GIVE WHAT YOU WANT TO RECEIVE

If you knew what I know about the power of giving, you would not let a single meal pass without sharing it in some way.

THE BUDDHA

*N*eeding, asking, getting—these are words we often use to describe our desires and the ways we try to fulfill them, but they have nothing to do with the way the universe works. The universe speaks a different language. The fact is that you don't get what you want from being greedy or needy. The universe is not interested in what you need, but in what you have to *give*.

Learning to give what you want to receive is the real secret of the law of attraction. When you are able to give the thing you want most, your inner being resonates with your wish in a new way, and you can recognize the forms in which the universe offers it to you. It's as though the "magnet" within you reverses its polarity; it now draws your desire to you, and you are ready to actually receive it.

●

The universe is not interested in what you need, but in what you have to give.

●

The less afraid we are of failing in life and not having what we want, the more willing we are to give of ourselves, both to life and to others. And not until we reach that point of willingness are we genuinely able to *receive*, from life or from others. Giving and receiving are not different things at all, but essentially the same thing: two aspects of the universal flow of energy. Within the universe, energy is constantly moving—giving and receiving, back and forth—and everything that happens in the universe is the result of this dynamic ebb and flow. Because you and the universe are constantly interacting with one another, stopping the flow has the same effect as a dam in a river: it blocks the vitality and energy in your life and your interaction with the universe dries up. This is what happens when you are not giving to life, but only looking to receive.

•

Giving and receiving are not two different things at all,
but essentially the same thing: two aspects of the
universal flow of energy.

•

The better you know yourself, the more you will discover that you can never receive what you yourself are unable to give. Thinking that you actually *can* smacks of a magical belief in some sort of *deus ex machina*—the erroneous assumption that you can be "saved" by something outside yourself, like a fairytale princess in a tower. But fairytales don't exist. Miracles, on the other hand, do exist, but they don't happen by themselves; that is, they don't happen to you unless you create the context for them to come about. And you do that by giving. If you want unconditional love, you must first learn to give unconditional love. If you want the perfect partner, you will have to become the partner you seek. If you want a sincere friendship, you will have to learn to be a friend.

Some time ago, I spoke to a woman who, like many of us, is always searching for that magical other half—the man who will make her happy, take care of her, and give her total security. She may well encounter this man on her path, but not before she is prepared to take care of herself in the same way she wants him to take care of her, and as a result is free to offer him the very same thing that she wants to receive from him. If she meets him before she has reached that point, she will not be able to receive what he offers.

●

You always receive exactly what you give in life,
or, to put it another way, you don't receive what you
don't give. Thus the ultimate responsibility for fulfilling
your desires lies with you.

●

Many of us are quick to feel disappointed or slighted when life does not give us what we want; we overlook our own role in creating our experience. We are so busy wanting, expecting, longing, and demanding that we don't stop to examine our wants, much less consider what we are willing to give. But you would do well to take this kind of close look at your desires, because what you expect from life and from others is exactly what you are unable to give yourself—and, therefore, anyone else. This means that the ultimate responsibility for fulfilling your desires lies quite literally with you. The universe works on the principle of cause and effect: you always receive exactly what you give in life, or, to put it another way, you don't receive what you don't give. The universe doesn't make one-sided deals. It unerringly senses if you want to receive more than you are willing to give. Everything is an exchange; nothing just drops out of the sky, though it may seem that way if you have not yet grasped the workings of the laws of creation or the power of your own unconscious processes.

•

The universe does not make one-sided deals.
It knows if you want to receive more
than you are willing to give.

•

Maybe you're now thinking, "Yes, but what if I want a new car (or new job or new house) right now? Do I have to be able to give it before I can get it? How is that possible?"

This brings me back to what I said in chapter 3 about how the universe works. The universe is energy, so it can only communicate with us energetically; it recognizes only the energy behind the material world and the energetic wish behind the material one. If you want a house, then of course it's probably not possible for you to give anyone else a house. To think of it this way makes no sense in the universe's terms. What is important is *why* you want the house—the energetic goal of the material wish. If the house represents inner peace, then that is what you are not yet able to give yourself. You will need to learn to offer peace—to yourself, to others, to life—before you will be able to receive it in any form, material or otherwise. And if there is no constructive goal behind your wish, the universe won't be able to help you.

I once saw an episode of *The Oprah Winfrey Show* in which Oprah experienced a magical moment with someone she had helped. She had given away a Porsche as a present to one of her readers. This man was extremely overweight, which meant that he could not fit into the

Porsche. To him, the car didn't represent money, status, or power. It stood for the self-esteem that he was going to have to summon in order to lose weight and allow himself to have a fit and healthy body. This is language that the universe does understand.

●

What is important is the energetic goal of the material wish. If that goal is inner peace then that is what you need to give before you can receive it.

●

The man wept when he finally got behind the wheel of his new car. It was a life-altering moment. Oprah said that she had never before experienced anything like what happened between her and that man at that moment. She felt as if she was a cog in the wheel of the universe.

This man had worked to be willing to give himself the self-esteem and self-respect he needed. And at the moment he fit into the car, he received that. The Porsche was just the effect; he had chosen to be the cause. He didn't decide to lose weight because he knew that he would get a high-end sports car as a reward. No, the gift was the effect of his decision to develop a healthy sense of self-esteem and to be true to himself in this. The Porsche was connected to an energetic wish that the universe understood completely. And because the universe does not respond to neediness, when the man no longer needed that Porsche, that was the moment when he at last received it.

Summary

- Learning to give what you want to receive is the true law of attraction.

- When you are able to give the thing you want most, it's as though your "magnet" reverses its polarity and you are ready to actually receive.

- If you want unconditional love, you must first learn to give unconditional love. If you want the perfect partner, you will have to become the partner you seek. If you want a sincere friendship, you will have to learn to be a friend.

- Giving and receiving are not two different things at all, but two aspects of the constant flow of energy in the universe.

- Because you and the universe are in constant interaction, stopping this dynamic flow of energy has the same effect as a dam in a river: it blocks the vitality and energy in your life and your interaction with the universe dries up.

- Everything is an exchange. Nothing just drops out of the sky, though it may seem that way if you have not yet grasped the power of your own unconscious processes.

- You always get back exactly what you give in life, and you don't receive what you don't give. The universe does not make one-sided deals. It unerringly senses if you want to receive more than you are willing to give.

Affirmation

---

*I am willing to give the things
I want to receive from life and from others.
I enter into an equal partnership with the universe.*

Practical Exercises

- On a sheet of paper or in your journal, make a list of the things you want in life and hope to receive from others. Make the list as specific and detailed as you can. If there are material wishes on your list, try to figure out what the energetic wishes behind those material desires are.

- Ask yourself whether you are really willing to give exactly the same things to others and to life that you desire and expect from them. Look at the list of wishes you've made. Are you able to give all these things? What do you need to do in order to be able to give them?

- Think of situations in which you feel needy or dependent. Whom do you feel dependent on? What are the things you need? How could you give yourself what you are seeking from others in those moments?

- Look at how often you are hurt, disappointed or deprived by people in your life, and examine in which ways you hurt, disappoint or deprive yourself and others—either consciously or unconsciously.

Law 12

KNOW YOUR
PURPOSE

The oldest wisdom in the world tells us that we can consciously join with the divine, while we find ourselves in this body; this is the reason for which man is truly born. If he misses his destination, then nature makes no haste; one day she will catch up and force him to fulfill her secret purpose.

SARVEPALLI RADHAKRISHNAN

President of India, 1962–7

*O*nce, after a lecture I had given on inner leadership, a man approached me. "You've been talking about focusing on your goal and connecting with your life purpose," he said. "But I wonder, is there really such as thing as a life purpose? I don't believe that everyone has a life purpose, and I'm wondering if it is all that important to find one."

•

Wanting to know why you're here and
what your life means is vital for being able to grow
mentally and spiritually.

•

Do we have a life purpose? I think so, and I'm certain that we need one to be truly happy. Without a purpose, life lacks meaning and you make decisions without passion. Because your choices are not anchored to a stable structure, they have short-lived but sometimes extreme effects, often bringing disappointment, sadness, and fear, along with chaos and disorder. People who are connected to their life's work, on the other hand, are easy to recognize. Their eyes shine because they are lit from within; their lives glow with enthusiasm and significance. They are bursting with energy because they nurture themselves rather than depending on others for their happiness and peace of mind. They often radiate serenity, and they are not easily swayed; their connection with their life's work gives them the power and the trust to get through difficult times and to enjoy the good ones. They see all that comes into their path in the light of their life's work, so they are good at discerning what is right for them and what is not.

●

For people without a purpose,
life can feel vague and empty. I never hear anyone say,
"Isn't it great that I don't know who I am or what I'm
here to do on earth?"

●

I meet many people who are not connected with their real life purpose, and they have no idea in which direction their lives should develop in any area—career, relationships, creative work. For these people, life feels like a puzzle full of missing pieces. They fumble around completely in the dark, confused about the meaning of everything. I never hear these people say, "Isn't it great that I don't know who I am or what I'm here to do on earth!" I don't know anyone who is really happy to go to sleep, get up, eat, work, and earn money without having the slightest notion what it's all for. Until the moment when you make the connection with your true purpose and begin allowing it to shape your life, your life can feel vague and empty. Wanting to know why you're here and what your life means is vital for being able to grow mentally and spiritually.

◦

If you don't know what your goal is in life,
then how can you create and atract what is right for you
and your path?

◦

A directionless life can have an enormously destructive effect on relationships as well, as people drag others into their discontent without intending or even noticing. I think that this is the reason for most divorces. The chronic restlessness and frustration that go hand-in-hand with not understanding one's purpose in life can put an enormous amount of strain on relationships. Some time ago, during my daily walk with my dog, I met a man about my age. He had a dog with him too, and we moved on down the path together as if we'd planned it that way. Although I was moving at a good clip and showing no interest in starting up a deep discussion, he began to talk very openly. He told me that he had collapsed at work the week before with palpitations and high blood pressure. His boss had advised him to stay at home for the time being, and his doctor had diagnosed incipient burnout.

The man started crying. "I'm sorry," he said. "It seems as if all I've been able to do all week is cry." As we walked, he explained that he was the head of the financial department in a large waste disposal company and had worked ever since he was young without ever really thinking about whether the work he did and the life he led were right for him. "I didn't feel unhappy, but I didn't feel happy either. I just carried on. And when I had two children with my wife, taking the time to figure out what I really wanted to do was no longer an option. There was no space for that." He started to cry again as he told me how guilty he felt towards his family. "I have a really fantastic wife whom I love very much," he said. "She's always there for me and is an incredibly good mother. But I've been so immersed in myself and am so busy trying to find inner peace and direction in life that if feels as if I don't have any room left inside to connect with her and my love for her."

❀

Not knowing your purpose in life
can have a destructive effect on your relationships as you
drag other people into your discontent.

❀

Maybe you, too, have always done what you thought was expected of you. Maybe you have tried to feel what you thought you were expected to feel both in work and relationships. It may be that you have no sense of any specific purpose in life, but just a vague feeling that you never do what you really want, never really dare to "go for it," or don't know your true self. Maybe you are no longer able to make choices that make you happy, that give you the feeling you are really alive.

●

Your unconscious knows exactly why you are here.
It speaks to you through your dreams, your intuition,
your deepest desires, and your hidden motives.

●

But your unconscious knows exactly why you are here. It can help you make choices that will let you give expression to your unique contribution to life. The key is to develop an ear and an eye for its messages. Your unconscious speaks to you through your dreams, your intuition, and your deepest desires; it reveals itself in your capabilities, your talents, and your hidden motives. And as long as you don't heed it, it will keep trying to get your attention, whispering to you—or maybe screaming at you—for as long as it takes you to hear and understand.

Its messages can take the form of restlessness, discontent, lack of energy, and even health problems. Caroline Myss writes about this in *Sacred Contracts*:

The lack of self-understanding and purpose in life is a health problem in itself in a certain sense, because it can lead to emotional stress, such as depression, fear and tiredness. And if these forms of stress or negative emotions become embedded, they can contribute to the development of an illness. Not only does your mind want to know your life's work, this knowledge is also of vital importance to your body and spirit. . . The further we stray from our life's work, the more frustrated we become and the more our energy becomes misaligned. Knowing your task in life enables you to lead your life in a way that makes the best use of your energy. When you manage your energy well, you also give the best expression to your personal power.

Not knowing your purpose in life can detract from your well-being in every area of your life, whether you are aware of it or not. The greatest harm is this: without direction, you cannot connect fully with your creative power, so the universe cannot help you as it should. To put the laws of creation to work for you, it's essential that you know your purpose. Throughout this book, we've been talking about creating and attracting what you wish for in your life, but if you don't know what your goal in life is, then how can you create and attract what is right for you and your path? How can you distinguish among the different events and experiences that come into your path, and what do you base your choices on? The power that is released when you know your life purpose includes the insight and trust that seemingly coincidental events—positive or negative—are never as random as they seem, but part of the subtle agenda of your soul, which offers you countless opportunities for growth and transformation.

◉

When you know your life purpose, you understand that the things that happen to you are not random, but part of the subtle agenda of your soul.

◉

I sincerely believe that a "life script" is mapped out for each of us before we're born, describing our task in this particular life. Equally, I'm convinced that each person is free to decide whether or not to follow that script. If you choose not to believe you have a life purpose, that's up to you. In my view, you don't *have* to have a purpose in order to live, but if you want to create, then you obviously *need* one. You need to know what you should focus on, and how you should direct your energy. After all, the goal determines the direction. Take athletes, for example. There isn't a single top cyclist who shows up for training saying,

"I guess I'll just start cycling and see what happens." No, he or she arrives with a goal in mind: to qualify for a certain event, to achieve a personal best, to be number one in the world.

●

You don't have to have a purpose,
but if you want to create, then you need one.

●

Many people love watching sports, which is why countless hours of TV time are devoted to it and why so much money is made from it. I'm convinced that this is because viewers like seeing people with clear goals, people who fight to rise from the ashes and achieve their dreams. Nearly everyone is inspired—or at least intrigued—by those who believe in something so strongly that they are willing to fail in order to eventually succeed, purely and simply as a result of knowing their purpose.

◉

No top cyclist shows up for training saying, "I don't have a goal. I'll just start cycling and see what happens."

◉

I've used athletic goals as an example, but our purpose in life cannot be derived solely from such outer things. When I talk about your true life purpose, I don't mean your work, your hobby, or your relationship alone. I mean, as Caroline Myss puts it, "your complete relationship with your personal and spiritual power." Finding your life purpose is not about making changes, big or small, to the institutional structures of your life. I have a good friend who is continually making changes of this kind in an attempt to quell his restlessness and find a measure of peace. A new house in another country, a new love, a new job to which he gives his all—until the restlessness and emptiness strike home and he must start all over again. He is looking in the wrong place for the cause of his restlessness, and this just leads him to doubt the meaning of his life even more.

◉

Your life's task is something that you bring into the world with you; you just have to remember it.

◉

No one can determine your purpose in life but you. In truth, finding out how to give expression to who you are at the deepest level is a process of *remembering* your purpose as much as discovering it. A train engineer once gave me a touching example of this. He heard me speak to a group of railroad employees about finding one's life purpose. A few months after the lecture, he wrote me: "The words you spoke gave me the impulse to do what I had always wanted. I started to use my appreciation for art in making knives inspired by the Celts, Picts, and Vikings."

He had enclosed some photographs of gorgeous hand-made knives with the most beautifully carved handles. The sensitivity of his work leapt out of the photos, but the significance was noticeable as well. Every piece he had created seemed to embody lifetimes. And when I recalled his face, I remembered that he even looked like a Celt.

I wrote back to him asking how he had discovered that this was what he needed to do with his life. He replied that he had talked with a friend, a doctor who was involved in genetic research, about how strange it is that we sometimes have skills that seem to be self-taught but cannot actually be so. "Like the fact that I can make almost anything with my hands that my mind's eye shows me." The doctor said, "That's actually not so strange, because we all have a genetic memory." Those words had struck the engineer. "I've always been interested in ancient peoples such as the Celts, Picts, and Vikings," he wrote to me. "That's how I know that a lot of Celtic archaeological sites can be found in the Belgian and French Ardennes. I love traveling there too." That had seemed like coincidence to him, but with the doctor's explanation of genetic memory in mind, he began to understand that it was part of remembering what he was meant to do.

He ended his letter with the perfect clue for coming into contact with one's life purpose. "I always listen to my feelings," he said simply. "I've been sharpening knives for over twenty-five years on Japanese whetstones using a technique that I learned as a young boy. About ten years ago, I started to make a knife for myself, just following my feeling of how to do it. It turned out so well that within a week I lost it to a friend who wanted to use it for outdoor sports. Then, after the impetus you gave me in your lecture and my friend's story about genetic memory, I started working one day a week less for the railroad and making knives part-time. I now sell my knives to people in Norway, South Africa, Belgium, Germany, and Scotland." He had sold one of the knives in the photo he sent me to a Scot who bought it as a wedding gift for his brother—"to cut the cake and to cut the babies' cords later on."

❧

Connecting with your life purpose means accepting that everything you do is for a reason far greater than you can comprehend.

❧

Your life's task is something that you bring into the world with you—you just have to remember it. You can do that by actively and courageously seeking it out. This sounds more mysterious than it is: if you are aligned with your life purpose, you can usually feel that you are on the right track, as the engineer did when he found that making knives resonated with his deepest being (and even with a memory older than his own life). During our lives, all of us go off track at one time or another—sometimes because we want to convince ourselves that we can abandon our task and choose an easier path that we think may bring us more fulfillment. But ignoring your life's task never leads to a more fulfilled life; in fact, your path may become even rougher in the long term, and you won't evade your task in the end. As Sarvepalli Radhakrishnan puts it, if you miss your destination, nature makes no haste; one day she will catch up and force you to fulfill her secret purpose.

●

When you act in alignment with your feelings, you will know when you come to a crossroads that involves the real purpose of your life.

●

Your ability to decipher your life's task depends first of all on your ability to perceive signs from the universe, the pointers that show whether or not you are on the right path. Finding your purpose has everything to do with learning to see the symbolic meaning of events, experiences, and relationships in your life. When you do, you can view events as part of a plan for your life in which you have a say. Looking at your life symbolically in this way gives you choice: the choice to see the things that happen to you either as accidents of fate or as pointers that the universe uses to redirect you and, in doing so, to remind you of your life's task. Look carefully at coincidental events or encouters. What messages do they contain? Which ones invite you to meet yourself on a deeper level, however uncomfortable it may seem at first? As with the Law of Redirection we discussed in chapter 1, if your life suddenly takes a completely different turn than you had expected or hoped, you can choose to regard this as the universe's way of getting your attention and steering you in the right direction for you.

Pay close attention to your conscience. This is another way your purpose speaks to you. When your conscience nags, if you examine your feelings carefully, you may discover that you are denying or repressing your higher potential. On the other hand, if you act from a place of truth, purity, love, and compassion, you'll have a feeling of peace, harmony, and well-being. Try to recognize when the universe is asking you to be of service. Don't ask yourself, "What do I want from life?" Ask yourself, "What does life want from me?" Don't think, "How can I get that thing I want?" Ask yourself instead, "What can I give of myself?"

Connecting with your purpose depends on your willingness to accept that everything you do is for a reason far greater than you can comprehend. You will not find your purpose by rational thinking alone, but by trusting your intuition and following your inner compass. When you take your feelings seriously and act in alignment with them, you will know when you come to a crossroads that involves the real purpose of your life. Have you ever had such an intense feeling about a person, a place, or a situation that the atmosphere actually changes—perhaps you have a sense of recognition, your thinking becomes clearer, your body reacts in a certain way, or a hint of sacredness hangs in the air? If so, you have connected with the part of your being that knows more about your true destiny than your conscious mind does.

●

Don't ask yourself, "What do I want from life?"
Ask yourself, "What does life want from me?"

●

What is your life purpose?

REQUIRED: *one curriculum vitae or resume. If you don't have one, you should make one now.*

Look at your CV or resume and carefully examine all your education and career choices. A CV represents each individual decision you have made in your studies and career, in addition to your movements from place to place—what we might call your material choices. But it also traces your emotional movements. Did you change your job because of a partner? Did you choose a course of study because of a parent's influence? Did you move to a new city for a new job or a promotion? What influences have other factors, such as children or your health, had on your CV? Have any of your life moves been intuitive choices, not based on specific considerations like a salary or a relationship—decisions you made because they just felt right?

You're about to make an analysis that you will want to write down. Draw the following three rows and three columns on a sheet of paper to create a grid with nine boxes. (You can also create this grid on your computer.) Label the columns according to the factors that drive your choices, intuitive, emotional, or material; then label each row according to the ways you make those choices. Are your decisions voluntary (a change you choose), involuntary (a change imposed on you), or unconscious (a course that you don't deliberately choose, but that arises from other actions you take or fail to take)?

	INTUITIVE CHOICES	EMOTIONAL CHOICES	MATERIAL CHOICES
VOLUNTARY DECISION			
INVOLUNTARY DECISION			
UNCONSCIOUS DECISION			

Yes, you can feel it coming: you're going to number each item on your CV, then place it in one of the nine boxes. Make the boxes really big so that you have lots of room for any explanations you want to add.

An item may need to go in more than one box. For example, moving is an emotional reason as well as a material reason for changing jobs. It may be a voluntary or an involuntary decision, but it's obviously not an unconscious decision! So you might place this job in as many as four boxes (emotional or material choice, voluntary or involuntary decision). If you took the new job because you moved to a new place, the explanation you write down is "moving," supplemented by the reason—"to new partner's town," for example.

If this were a quiz in a magazine, there would be a key you could consult to tally your "score" and interpret the results. *(Give yourself one point for each voluntary intuitive choice...)* But this exercise is not about the outcome. The process of analysis you go through to correctly place each CV item in the grid is all the result you need. It is an exercise designed to slow down your thinking so that you can gain better insight into your own feelings and thought processes and the effects these have had on your decisions. As you work through the exercise, you may see a pattern emerge, and this pattern may give you insight into the purpose behind your path.

Summary

- Without a purpose, your life lacks meaning and you make decisions without passion. Your choices are often accompanied by disappointment, disorder, sadness, and fear.

- A lack of understanding of your life purpose can have a destructive effect in every area of your life, whether you are aware of it or not.

- Wanting to know why you are here and what your life means is vital for your growth, both spiritually and mentally, and so you can find real fulfillment and peace of mind.

- Finding your purpose is not about making changes, big or small, to the outward circumstances of your life. Rather, it is about giving expression to who you are at the very deepest level.

- When you live a life without direction, you cannot connect fully to your creative power, so the universe cannot help you create and attract what is right for you and your path in life. To put the laws of creation to work for you, you must know your purpose.

Affirmation

I give my life sense and meaning by knowing my true purpose. I choose the goal that best enables me to express my personal and spiritual power.

In Practice

- If you haven't yet worked through the "What Is Your Life Purpose?" exercise at the end of this chapter, go back and try it now. What have you discovered about the way you make your choices? Do you see a pattern or begin to get a sense of the purpose that is guiding you?

- Try to recall the moments in your life in which you have felt the greatest sense of direction and purpose. What were you doing at that time? Where were you? Were you with others or alone? And what exactly was it that gave you such a good feeling?

- Ask yourself whether the life you are leading now is an expression of your personal and spiritual power. If you don't think it is, what is holding you back from being who you are at the deepest level of your being? What is holding you back from living the life that is a reflection of this?

- The universe gives you signs, such as "coincidental" encounters, and your unconscious speaks to you in dreams, through your intuition, and through your deepest desires to bring you into contact with your life purpose. Take some time to think about any signs you may be receiving.

- Set two goals for a specific period of time—a month, two months, a year—to help you be the person you want to be and create the life that is right for you. Write down these goals and focus on the feeling that achieving them will bring you. When you have reached these goals, you can write down two more to bring you closer still to the life you want.

- Look at the skills, qualities, and talents you already have to enable you to achieve the goals you've written down. Think about what other skills and talents you will need to develop. Promise yourself that you will summon the self-discipline and integrity necessary to realize your dreams.

THE DEEPER
SECRET MEDITATION

*L*earn to know yourself, reflect on what you want, and connect with your life purpose by turning your thoughts inwards positively and honestly, without judgment.

Choose a moment of quietness. Sit in a relaxed position on the floor, on a cushion, or on a chair that is about the same height as a dining-room chair. If you are sitting on the floor or on a cushion, sit in the lotus position or simply cross-legged. If you are sitting on a chair, put your feet side by side on the floor, hold your back and shoulders straight, and let your hands rest in your lap. Withdraw from the outside world and concentrate on your breathing. Breathe in through your nose and hold this for a moment. Then breathe out through your mouth, exhaling for longer than you normally would and letting the air flow out between your slightly open lips without pursing them or exhaling too hard. When outside thoughts intrude, bring your focus back to your breathing.

With every in-breath, focus on breathing in the qualities you need for your personal development, such as courage, willpower, and perseverance. With every out-breath, focus on letting go of the aspects of your personality that create obstacles to realizing your goal and keep you from being your true self, such as fear, doubt, or insecurity. When you are ready—which may be after a few meditative moments or not until you've done several sessions—it's time for you to focus your energy on whatever constructive goal you have chosen. Maybe you're seeking clarity about why you want what you want, working on being present in the here and now, letting go of negative thoughts to create space for trust, or discerning the purpose of your life. Focus on how that goal feels.

Do this for five minutes or more, every day or several times a week. If this kind of practice is new to you, give yourself time to get used to it. If you're someone who likes to draw fast conclusions and act quickly, you may find it frustrating at first and feel like nothing is happening, but don't let yourself get discouraged. If you keep practicing, you will get results really quickly, and you'll start to see the purpose of the exercises more clearly.

AFTERWORD

*Y*ou have the power to create the life you want, the life you were meant to live. But working with the laws of creation and connecting with your own creative power takes practice and it takes time. It's not a trick that you can master just by reading a book or attending a workshop. It is a spiritual path on which willingness is a necessary condition—the willingness to do the inner work that life challenges you with in all events and encounters. This is not a path of asking and getting; it is a path of learning to give and receive. It is a journey to surrender, faith, trust, and above all, gratitude: gratitude for life as it is now and for the opportunities that you are offered in the Now.

This book did not land on your path by coincidence. It is time for you to stop seeing power and strength everywhere except in yourself. It is time to look within, to bring your limiting thoughts and beliefs to light and then put them behind you. It is time to stop seeing your life as a series of random happenings with you as their defenseless victim. Your life is exactly as it should be now. Everything is as it should be now, because the entire universe is as it should be. Once you understand fully and clearly that you create your circumstances with your thoughts, beliefs, and feelings and that you are not at the mercy of an unpredictable fate, then, instead of running from reality, you can use it as a map that shows exactly where you are on your journey and how you can move forward.

This book is a tribute to your courage and creative power and a tribute to the logic and love of the universe.

BIBLIOGRAPHY

Bancroft, Anne. *Women in Search of the Sacred*. New York: Penguin, 1997.

Myss, Caroline. *Sacred Contracts*. New York: Three Rivers Press, 2003.

Pierrakos, Eva. *The Pathwork of Self-Transformation*. New York: Bantam, 1990.

Postma, Annemarie. *Ik hou van mij*. Amsterdam: Forum, 2007.

Postma, Annemarie. *Liefde maken*. Amsterdam: Forum, 2007.

Stolp, Hans. *Kijken met de ogen van je hart*. Kampen: Ten Have, 2004.

Tolle, Eckhart. *The Power of Now*. Novato, CA: New World Library, 2004.